BAKING WITH MARIAN

By Marian Getz

www.cookbookdesigner.com

Printed in the U.S.A.

Acknowledgements

Thank you, Wolfgang, for allowing me to cook with you. You have shared your stage with me while making me laugh and feel welcomed. There is no other chef in the world that I would rather work for.

To my husband Greg, whose passion for great food and endless encouragement are the real reason I cook. I love you, honey. It has been a delicious life so far.

To Jordan, Lindsay and Benjamin, I simply love you.

To all my boy's friends who I have fed over the years, it's been a privilege and joy to have the home that is the "neighborhood hangout". You are always welcome.

To Mom, for inviting me into the kitchen and not noticing when I made a mess.

To Dad, your generous praise is why I couldn't wait to get into the kitchen to bake for you when I was little.

To Phyllis, Alan, Marla, Susanna, Dottie and all my dear friends who were there in the early Ottawa days, encouraging me and fueling my budding desire to feed people food that tastes delicious. In part, because of you, my dream came true.

When you are lucky enough to work for Wolfgang Puck, you are also ever so fortunate to work with the likes of Sydney Silverman, Jonathan Schwartz, Mike Sanseverino, Arnie Simon, Phoebe Soong, Nicolle Brown and many other wonderful people at the office. Special thanks to Daniel Koren for your gentle patience and turning my garbled words and scribbled recipes into a sweet story. A special thanks goes out to Daniel as well for the beautiful photographs that make this book so special. You have taken my humble food and captured it on film so that each photo makes me hungry.

A special thank you to the HSN customers, for your loyalty and commitment to my books.

Throughout my career as a chef, I have always held the world of desserts and pastries in high regard. Perhaps this is a result of my rather large sweet tooth. It may also be because dessert is the last course of a meal and you want your guests to end their dining experience on a positive note. Marian is one of the best at presenting delicious and fascinating desserts. Her new book will empower you to duplicate these results at your dinner table.

I have had the pleasure of working with Marian for more than 11 years . Her passion and dedication to cooking, especially baking, has only grown stronger. In addition to being very loyal and hard working, she is truly a student of her craft.

Marian's new baking book really showcases her talent in the best light possible. The manner in which she presents the recipes truly reflects her ability to pass on her knowledge. I feel it is important not only to be an exceptional cook, but also willing to teach others what you have learned along the way. Marian does both beautifully and with great passion.

Every kitchen needs a good collection of cookbooks that cover a wide variety of foods. Marian's baking book is a wonderful addition to your book pantry.

Wolfgang Puck

Table Of Contents

Cakes & Pastries
Page 10

Cookies & Bars
Page 40

Pies & Such

Crackers, Breads & Pizzas

More

Fillings & Toppings

Baking Tips

There are 4 major components to achieving great baking results:

1) Accurate Measuring
2) Great tools
3) Understanding your oven and its temperature accuracy
4) Accurate Timing

Accurate Measuring

Accurate measuring is critical to achieving success in baking. Use glass measuring cups for liquid ingredients and metal measuring cups for dry ingredients. The measuring spoons I prefer are long and narrow so they will fit in the neck of a spice jar.

I recommend measuring in piles to keep track of ingredients. For example, in a mixing bowl, add the flour, then a separate pile of sugar, a separate pile of baking powder, etc. This allows you to review the ingredients you have already used and keep track of what needs to be added. If you mix all the ingredients together, you will be more likely to forget ingredients which will result in an undesired outcome and may discourage you from baking in the future.

Salt

The salt used for the recipes in this book is Diamond Crystal Kosher Salt. It is half as salty as most other brands. The grains are very fluffy and thus not as many fit into a measuring spoon. Also, this brand lists "salt" as the only ingredient on the box. If you are using a different brand, simply use half the amount specified in the recipe.

Chocolate / Cocoa

Buy good quality chocolate and cocoa. While it is easy to find excellent chocolate at most grocery stores, it is almost impossible to find good cocoa powder. Check the source page in the back of the book to find quality cocoa.

Vanilla

I order both my vanilla extract and beans from a supplier on the island of Tahiti. Tahitian extract and beans are my favorite. I use both in recipes where the vanilla flavor takes center stage. In recipes where vanilla is not the main flavor, like lemon cake, I use imitation vanilla because it adds the correct taste and aroma but is far less expensive. I also like an inexpensive imitation flavoring called Magic Line Butter Vanilla Extract. It adds an incredible sweet smell to baked goods and its aroma reminds me of how a really good bakery smells.

Butter

All of the butter used in this book is unsalted. Softened butter means butter that has been left at room temperature for several hours. It should be soft enough to offer no resistance when sliced with a knife. While there is no substitute for the pure flavor of butter, you can use a butter alternatives such as margarine in most of the recipes. You will still achieve great baking results.

Sugar Substitute

If you need to use a sugar substitute, my favorite kind is an all natural product called Zsweet. I get it at my local health food store. While it does not bake as perfectly as regular sugar, it is the best substitute that I know of.

Be Organized

Read through the recipe once then gather all the ingredients before you start to measure and prepare the recipe.

Use Caution

Use caution when dealing with hot baked goods. I suggest using a pair of hand mitts or pot holders to avoid any burns.

Even Baking

Rotate the baking sheets from top to bottom and turn the trays halfway in the middle of the baking cycle to ensure even baking.

Avoid Stickiness

To avoid sticking, use parchment paper, non-stick spray or silicone-coated aluminum foil.

Testing for Doneness

When baking cakes, test for doneness by inserting a toothpick or a bamboo skewer off center into the cake. When the toothpick is removed, it should have just a few moist crumbs on it. For custards, insert a knife off center and when removed, it should come out clean. For breads, bake until the internal temperature is 200 degrees on a thermometer. For cookies, pizzas and pastries look for slight puffing and a golden brown color.

For more of Marian's tips and ideas, please visit:
www.mariangetz.com

Tools

1. Wooden Spoon
2. Pastry Brush
3. Ultra Thin Flexible Spatula
4. Whisk
5. Peeler
6. Pastry Wheel
7. Digital Thermometer
8. Small Paring Knife
9. Narrow Measuring Spoons
10. Digital Timer
11. Citrus Grater
12. Mini Blow Torch
13. Ice Cream Scoop
14. French Cake Rack
15. Cheesecloth Bag with Dry Beans as Pie Weights
16. Hand Mixer
17. Hand Mixer Attachments
18. Cookie Press
19. Cookie Press Attachments

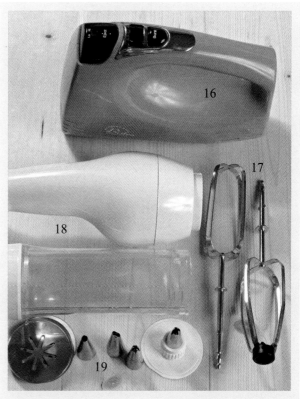

Cakes & Pastries

New York Crumb Cake

Makes 1 cake

Cake Ingredients

½ cup granulated sugar
1¼ cups cake flour
¼ teaspoon baking soda
½ teaspoon kosher salt
6 tablespoons unsalted butter, softened
1 large egg
1 large egg yolk
2 teaspoons vanilla extract
⅓ cup buttermilk

Topping

1¾ cups cake flour
½ cup unsalted butter, melted
¼ teaspoon kosher salt
¼ teaspoon ground cinnamon
⅓ cup granulated sugar
⅓ cup light brown sugar, packed

I have to admit that whenever I eat this cake, I shamelessly nibble off all the crumbs and leave the cake part behind. I am a sucker for anything resembling a crumble or streusel type topping. This recipe is one of my favorites because it is the one cake in the world where you are supposed to have a higher crumb-to-cake ratio. Don't make the mistake of using all purpose flour in place of the cake flour. It is the secret to the tender cake and crumbs. The hint of cinnamon puts this cake over the top.

1. Preheat oven to 325 degrees; grease an 8x8-inch square pan.

2. In the bowl of a stand mixer fitted with the beaters, combine the sugar, flour, baking soda and salt. Mix on medium speed, add the butter followed by the remaining cake ingredients and mix for 3 minutes or until smooth.

3. Scrape the mixture into the prepared square pan and smooth out the batter.

4. In a bowl, combine all topping ingredients; mix with your fingers then toss until a solid dough forms.

5. Gently break the dough into grape-size pieces.

6. Scatter topping pieces over the batter in the pan then bake for 40 minutes or until well browned; test for doneness using a toothpick (only a few moist crumbs should stick to the toothpick).

7. Dust with powdered sugar and serve warm.

Honey Snails

Makes 15 snails

Ingredients

2 packages (8 ounces each) cream cheese, warmed
⅓ cup granulated sugar
1 box (16 ounces) phyllo dough, thawed

2 cups unsalted butter, melted
⅔ cup honey

1. Preheat oven to 350 degrees.

2. Line a rimmed cookie sheet with parchment paper; set aside.

3. In a bowl, combine the cream cheese and sugar; mix until smooth.

4. Transfer cream cheese mixture to a pastry bag; set aside.

5. Unroll phyllo dough onto a damp towel and cover it with another damp towel to prevent it from drying out.

6. Place a sheet of phyllo dough on the counter and lightly brush it with butter.

7. Top with another sheet of phyllo dough and brush it with butter as well.

8. Repeat with another layer of phyllo dough and butter it to make a 3rd layer.

9. Pipe a 1/2-inch thick band of the cream cheese mixture along one of the long sides of the dough.

10. Roll up the dough over the filling then coil the roll similar to a cinnamon roll.

11. Place rolls on the cookie sheet and brush them with additional butter.

12. Repeat to make additional rolls.

13. Bake for 25-30 minutes or until golden brown and crispy.

14. Top the snails with honey while hot and serve.

Lanier's
Tupelo
Honey

Best Sticky Buns

Makes 15 buns

Buns

1 envelope active dry yeast
¼ cup lukewarm water
½ cup whole milk
4 large eggs

4 cups unbleached all purpose flour, divided
⅓ cup granulated sugar
½ cup unsalted butter, softened
1 teaspoon kosher salt

Filling

4 tablespoons unsalted butter, melted
2 teaspoons vanilla extract
1 cup light brown sugar, packed
1 tablespoon ground cinnamon
½ cup dark raisins

Sticky Pan Bottom

2 tablespoons unsalted butter, softened
½ cup maple syrup
2 cups pecan halves
Pinch of kosher salt

1. In the bowl of a stand mixer fitted with the dough hook, combine yeast and water; let stand for 5 minutes then mix on low speed while adding the milk and eggs.

2. Add 1 cup of flour, mix on medium speed for 2 minutes then add 2 cups of flour, sugar, butter and salt. Mix for 2 minutes then add remaining flour. Mix for 3 minutes until a smooth but sticky dough forms; cover with a towel and let it rise for 1 hour.

3. On a lightly floured surface, punch the dough down, knead it into a ball and flatten it into a thick rectangle; cover with a towel and let rest for 15 minutes.

4. In a bowl, combine all filling ingredients; mix well and set aside.

5. For the sticky pan bottom, grease a 9x13-inch baking pan with butter, pour in the syrup then top with pecans and salt.

6. Pat dough into a large rectangle, spread filling, roll it up and pinch the edges.

7. Cut into 15 rolls and place them into the pan; cover and let rest for 1 hour.

8. Bake at 350 degrees for 45 minutes or until dark brown; let rest for 5 minutes then invert onto a serving plate and serve warm.

Dutch Baby

Makes 2 - 4 servings

Ingredients

¾ cup all purpose flour
¾ cup whole milk
3 large eggs
½ teaspoon kosher salt

3 tablespoons unsalted butter
3 cups mixed fresh berries
Maple syrup
Powdered sugar

A Dutch Baby is quick and inexpensive to make yet so delicious. It is a pancake that puffs up dramatically in the hot oven. It is crispy, comforting and begs to be drenched in maple syrup. My children are grown now but still get excited whenever I make this dish. It is fun to watch through the oven glass as the pancake puffs and makes a giant bowl-shaped confection of crispy-chewy goodness.
Since it falls quickly once removed from the oven, you need to be ready to eat it the moment it comes out of the oven.

1. Preheat oven to 450 degrees.

2. In a bowl, combine flour, milk, eggs and salt; whisk well using an immersion blender and set aside.

3. Slide the oven rack to the upper 1/3 of the oven.

4. Place a 10-inch omelet pan with sloped sides on the oven rack and let it heat up for 10 minutes.

5. Carefully pull the oven rack out and add the butter to the omelet pan; close the oven door and let the butter melt for 3 minutes.

6. Carefully pull the oven rack out and pour the batter into the center of the pan; avoid splashing the batter.

7. Bake for 20-25 minutes or until puffed into a bowl shape and deep brown in color.

8. Remove from oven using heavy pot holders and set it on a heat-proof surface.

9. Pour berries into the center, top with syrup and dust with powdered sugar.

10. Serve immediately.

Cream Puffs

Makes 12 servings

Ingredients

1 cup water

¼ cup unsalted butter

1 teaspoon kosher salt

1 teaspoon granulated sugar

1 cup bread flour

1 teaspoon baker's ammonia, optional (see source page)

4 large eggs

2 large egg whites, divided

Quick Strawberry Mousse Filling (see page 137)

Powdered sugar for dusting

1. Line two 1/4 sheet pans with aluminum foil; set aside.

2. In a large saucepan, combine water, butter, salt and sugar; bring to a boil.

3. Add the flour to the saucepan; stir vigorously using a wooden spoon for 1 minute or until a solid dough ball forms.

4. Using a hand mixer on medium speed, beat in the ammonia, eggs and 1 egg white until a smooth and a uniform color is achieved; scrape the sides.

5. To test if the dough needs another egg white, pinch a bit of the dough between your thumb and index finger. Pull your fingers apart. If the dough stretches out in a strand 2 inches long, no additional egg white is needed. Mix in the remaining egg white if you can't stretch a 2-inch strand of dough.

6. Scoop or pipe six 2-inch dough balls onto each sheet pan.

7. Sprinkle dough ball tops with droplets of water to pat down any points.

8. Preheat oven to 425 degrees.

9. Bake for 20 minutes then reduce the oven temperature to 350 degrees.

10. Bake for an additional 30 minutes or until puffs triple in size and are deep brown in color.

11. Remove and let cool before filling them with the Quick Strawberry Mousse filling and dusting them with powdered sugar.

Vienna Pastry Cake

Ingredients

1 Vienna Pastry Pie Crust, unbaked (see page 67)
2 cups heavy cream
½ cup granulated sugar
½ teaspoon pure vanilla extract
4 cups fresh mixed fruits

Here I turned my often used Vienna Pastry Pie Crust recipe into a layer cake. The contrast between the crispy-tender crust and the soft cream is remarkable. Layering the pastry with the whipped cream and fruit creates a stunning cake with very little effort.

1. Preheat oven to 350 degrees.

2. Line 2 cookie sheets with parchment paper.

3. On a lightly floured surface, roll out the dough from the Vienna Pastry Pie Crust into four 6-inch circles (1/4-inch thick) and place them on the cookie sheets.

4. Bake for 20 minutes or until golden brown.

5. Remove and let cool.

6. In a bowl, combine cream, sugar and vanilla; whip using a hand mixer until stiff peaks form.

7. Spread each dough circle with 1 cup of cream mixture and desired fruits.

8. Stack each layer to create a 4-layer cake.

9. Top with desired fruit and serve within 2 hours.

Marian's Tip:
If you're short on time, just use a store-bought pie crust.

Napoleons

Makes 12 servings

Ingredients

1 package (17.3 ounces) puff pastry sheets, frozen
Pastry Cream (see page 125)
Vanilla Glaze (see page 136)
Chocolate Glaze (see page 136)

1. Preheat oven to 375 degrees.

2. Line 2 sheet pans with parchment paper.

3. Thaw 1 sheet of puff pastry and unfold it onto one of the sheet pans.

4. Cut the puff pastry in half lengthwise and move it so the sides are not touching.

5. Cover the puff pastry pieces with a sheet of parchment paper.

6. Place the second sheet pan on top of the pastry to act as a weight during baking.

7. Bake for 20 minutes or until evenly puffed and light brown.

8. Remove the top sheet pan and bake for an additional 5 minutes or until dark brown.

9. Let cool completely.

10. Transfer half of the baked puff pastry sheet to a serving tray.

11. Top with pastry cream then place the second half of the puff pastry sheet on top.

12. Gently press to level and even out.

13. Spoon the vanilla glaze over the top and spread it just over the edges.

14. Use a piece of parchment paper to make a parchment piping bag and fill it with 1/2 cup of chocolate glaze.

15. Pipe lines with the chocolate glaze on top of the vanilla glaze.

16. Use a toothpick to draw decorative lines through both icings before they dry.

17. Let rest for 20 minutes then trim the uneven edges with a serrated knife.

18. Cut into small bars and serve.

Raspberry Empress Cake

Makes 1 cake

Ingredients

4 large eggs
1 teaspoon baking powder
1 teaspoon kosher salt
¾ cup sugar
1 teaspoon pure vanilla extract

¾ cup cake flour, sifted
1¼ cups good quality raspberry jam
Additional sugar for sprinkling
2 quarts vanilla ice cream, softened
Raspberry Coulis (see page 137)

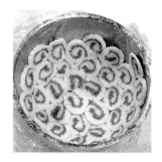

1. Preheat oven to 400 degrees.

2. Apply flour-flavored non-stick spray to two 1/4 sheet pans; set aside.

3. In the bowl of a stand mixer fitted with the whisk attachment, combine eggs, baking powder and salt; beat on high for 3 minutes or until light and fluffy.

4. Reduce speed to medium and continue to beat while slowly adding the sugar.

5. Increase the speed to high and continue to beat for 8 minutes or until pale yellow and thick.

6. Fold in the vanilla using a rubber spatula and slowly add the flour in batches.

7. Divide the batter between the two sheet pans; nudge batter into any bare spots.

8. Bake for 12 minutes; test for doneness by pressing a finger on the cake. If it springs back, it is done.

9. Tear off 2 sheets of plastic wrap, each a few inches longer than the sheet pan; apply non-stick spray to the sheets and sprinkle with sugar.

10. Invert cakes onto the prepared foil sheets and lift off the pans.

11. Stir the jam then spread it evenly over the cakes.

12. Roll up each cake tightly starting with one of the long sides. Roll each in another sheet of plastic wrap then place them in the freezer for 2 hours.

13. To make the mold, line a curved bowl or sauté pan with plastic wrap.

14. Remove jelly rolls from the freezer and slice them into 1/4-inch thick slices.

15. Place a slice in the center of the mold then add slices in a spiral pattern, pressing them close together all the way up the sides of the bowl.

16. Fill the mold to the top with ice cream then cover and freeze for several hours; invert onto a serving tray and serve with raspberry coulis.

Apple Cider Cake with Apple Icing

Makes 1 cake

Cake Ingredients

1½ cups unbleached all purpose flour
2 teaspoons baking powder
½ teaspoon kosher salt
⅔ cup apple cider
2 teaspoons fresh lemon juice
½ cup unsalted butter
1 cup granulated sugar
3 large eggs
¼ teaspoon ground cinnamon

Apple Icing

¾ cup granulated sugar
3 tablespoons cornstarch
⅛ teaspoon kosher salt
¾ cup apple cider
1¼ cups unsalted butter

The unusual icing in this recipe is what drew me to it in the beginning. It uses a cooked base. The only other recipe that I know of that begins the icing in this manner is red velvet cake icing. It is incredibly delicious and light on the tongue. The same is true for the cake, and when you put both together, it is just so right. If you are lucky enough to find unfiltered apple cider at your market, the cake will turn out even better.

1. Preheat oven to 350 degrees.

2. Grease two 8-inch round cake pans; set aside.

3. In a bowl, combine flour, baking powder, and salt; set aside.

4. In a measuring cup, combine apple cider and lemon juice; set aside.

5. In a large mixing bowl, combine butter and sugar; beat using a hand mixer until light and fluffy.

6. While beating, add eggs (one at a time) to the butter mixture (the mixture will look curdled).

7. While continuing to beat, add the flour mixture and apple cider mixture in batches to the butter mixture until smooth.

8. Divide the mixture between the two cake pans.

9. Bake for 25-30 minutes; test for doneness using a toothpick.

10. Allow cake to cool then refrigerate for 4 hours or until cold.

11. To make the icing, combine sugar, cornstarch and salt in a 2-quart heavy saucepan.

12. Whisk in the apple cider and bring it to a boil over medium heat; whisk constantly until mixture becomes very thick.

13. Transfer the mixture to a mixing bowl and place the bowl into a larger bowl holding ice cold water.

14. Stir occasionally until cool (about 30 minutes).

15. In a separate bowl, beat the butter using a hand mixer until light and fluffy.

16. Pour cider mixture into the butter and mix on high until light and smooth.

17. Ice the tops of each cake layer with the cider-butter mixture, stack and serve.

Pineapple Upside Down Cake

Makes 1 cake

Ingredients

3 tablespoons unsalted butter, softened
4 tablespoons light brown sugar, packed
14 pineapple slices, ½-inch thick, core removed
14 fresh cherries

Batter

⅔ cup granulated sugar
¼ cup unsalted butter, softened
1 large egg
⅔ cup pineapple juice
2 teaspoons vanilla extract
2 teaspoons baking powder
1⅓ cups unbleached all purpose flour

This is the exact pineapple upside down cake you see Wolfgang pull out of the oven during the cookware segments on HSN. The heavily buttered pan is the secret to "anchoring" the pineapple slices and cherries in place as the batter is poured over. Now you know the secret recipe.

Marian's Tip:
If you don't have fresh cherries, the maraschino jarred variety are a great substitute.

1. Preheat oven to 350 degrees.

2. Grease the bottom and sides of a 8-inch round cake pan with 3 tablespoons of butter and sprinkle brown sugar across the pan; twirl pan until the butter is evenly coated with sugar.

3. Press the pineapple slices evenly across the bottom and sides of the pan into the butter.

4. Press a cherry into the center of each pineapple slice.

5. In a bowl, combine all batter ingredients; mix well using a whisk until smooth.

6. Pour batter into the pineapple-lined pan and smooth out the top using a rubber spatula.

7. Bake for 25-30 minutes; test for doneness using a tooth pick.

8. Let cool for 10 minutes then loosen the edges with a table knife and invert the cake onto a plate.

1-2-3 Cheesecake

Makes 1 cake

Ingredients
1 pound cream cheese, softened
2 cups granulated sugar
3 large eggs

I developed this recipe for a story in the magazine "Better Homes & Gardens" that was written about me for their "Cooks We Love" segment.
I adore cheesecake and over the years I pared down the ingredient list to the bare elements. This is pure cheesecake at its best. I always bake my cheesecakes crustless like this. If I want a crunchy element, I serve it with buttery shortbread cookies. I also love to serve this with my homemade jams as a topping. This recipe is very easy to remember:

1-2-3
1 pound cream cheese
2 cups sugar
3 eggs

1. Preheat oven to 300 degrees.

2. Place the cream cheese in a microwave-safe bowl.

3. Microwave for 1 minute.

4. Transfer the cream cheese to a food processor and add the sugar; process until smooth.

5. Scrape the sides of the food processor and process for an additional 1 minute.

6. Add the eggs to the food processor and process for 5 seconds.

7. Scrape the bowl and process for an additional 5 seconds.

8. Apply non-stick spray to a 9-inch round cake pan.

9. Pour batter into the pan and smooth the top.

10. Set up a water bath by filling a 10-inch round pan with 1 inch of very hot water and placing the 9-inch pan into the water bath; place in the oven.

11. Bake for 30 minutes, rotating the pan after 15 minutes; bake for an additional 30 minutes, let cool for 1 hour at room temperature then chill for 8 hours before serving.

Cream Cheese Baby Cakes

Makes about 10 baby cakes

Ingredients

4 ounces cream cheese, softened
¾ cup (1½ sticks) unsalted butter, softened
1½ cups granulated sugar
3 large eggs

1 teaspoon pure vanilla extract
½ teaspoon kosher salt
1½ cups unbleached all purpose flour

If I only allowed myself to lick one kind of batter off the end of a spoon, this would be the one. The taste is vanilla-sweet and softly flavored with that unmistakable cream cheese tang. This also makes the very best pound cake recipe when baked. The original is a David Waltuck creation from his wonderful New York restaurant called Chanterelle. You can easily "morph" this into a different flavor by adding toasted nuts, dried fruits, chocolate chips or citrus zest. Make sure you use the highest quality pure vanilla extract you can find. It will make a huge difference.

1. Preheat oven to 325 degrees.

2. In a bowl, combine cream cheese, butter and sugar; cream using a mixer until fluffy.

3. Add eggs to the bowl and mix until incorporated.

4. Scrape the sides of the bowl then add remaining ingredients; mix until just smooth.

5. Scrape the batter into greased baby cake or mini loaf pans until 3/4 full.

6. Bake for 25 minutes or until golden brown; use a toothpick to test for doneness.

7. Let cool for 20 minutes before removing from the pans.

Marian's Tip:
If you have any cakes leftover, don't worry because they freeze very well.

Coconut Layer Cake

Makes 1 cake

Ingredients

½ cup unsalted butter, softened
½ cup solid white shortening
1 tablespoon baking powder
1¾ cups granulated sugar
1 teaspoon kosher salt
2 teaspoons vanilla extract

1 tablespoon coconut extract
5 large egg whites
2¾ cups cake flour, divided
1 cup canned coconut milk, divided
Swiss Meringue (see page 132)
Real Toasted Coconut (see page 127)

1. Preheat oven to 350 degrees.

2. Butter and flour two 8-inch round cake pans; set aside.

3. In a bowl, combine butter, shortening, baking powder, sugar, salt, vanilla and coconut extracts; cream using a hand mixer for 5 minutes or until fluffy.

4. Scrape the bowl, add the egg whites and beat well; scrape the bowl again.

5. Add half of the flour to the bowl, mix then add half of the milk and mix well.

6. Repeat with remaining flour and coconut milk.

7. Divide the batter evenly between the cake pans.

8. Bake for 20-25 minutes; test for doneness using a toothpick (when inserted in the center, only a few moist crumbs should stick to the toothpick).

9. Let cool completely before cutting the layers in half.

10. Frost the layers with Swiss Meringue.

11. Top with coconut and serve.

Best White Cake

Makes two 8-inch layers

Ingredients

1¾ cups granulated sugar

½ cup unsalted butter, softened

½ cup solid white shortening

1 teaspoon kosher salt

1 tablespoon baking powder

1 teaspoon vanilla extract

¼ teaspoon butter-vanilla extract

⅛ teaspoon almond extract

5 large egg whites

2¾ cups cake flour, divided

1 cup whole milk, divided

I usually prefer yellow cake to white cake but this recipe is different and I really like it. The color is gorgeous. I get asked to make so many wedding cakes that I had to find a white cake recipe that is both yummy and reliable. This recipe is always perfect and is not too much trouble to put together. The trick to making a nice looking cake is to start early and always ice a cake that is very cold so it is sturdier and does not produce crumbs.

*Marian's Tip:
Ice this cake with the Seven Minute Frosting on page 130.*

1. Preheat oven to 350 degrees.

2. Butter and flour two 8-inch round pans; set aside.

3. In the bowl of a stand mixer fitted with the paddle attachment, combine sugar, butter, shortening, salt and baking powder.

4. Mix on medium for 5 minutes then scrape the bowl.

5. Add the extracts and egg whites to the bowl; mix well.

6. While mixing on low, add the flour and milk in batches until all is added.

7. Blend until batter is uniform in color; don't overmix.

8. Divide batter evenly between the two round pans.

9. Bake for 20-25 minutes; test for doneness using a toothpick.

10. Let cool for 10 minutes before removing from pans.

Vanilla Angel Food Cake

Makes 1 cake

Ingredients

1 cup cake flour
1½ cups granulated sugar, divided
1¾ cups large egg whites (from about 13 eggs)
1 tablespoon water

¼ teaspoon kosher salt
½ teaspoon cream of tartar
Seeds from ½ of a vanilla bean

Most of us enjoy angel food cake, but not too many people know how to make one from scratch. The difference between store bought and homemade angel food cake is like the difference between canned peaches and fresh peaches. There really is no comparison. This recipe truly showcases the vanilla bean. Not only does it create an unforgettable taste, but the way the vanilla bean seeds are suspended throughout the cake adds to the dramatic presentation.

Marian's Tip:
The stand mixer bowl and beaters need to be perfectly clean to make this recipe.

1. Preheat oven to 350 degrees.

2. In a bowl, sift flour and 3/4 cup of sugar; sift a second time then set aside.

3. In the clean bowl of a stand mixer fitted with clean beaters, combine remaining ingredients, except vanilla bean seeds and remaining sugar.

4. Beat for 2 minutes on medium speed or until foamy then increase the speed to high.

5. While beating, slowly add the remaining sugar and beat for 4 minutes or until soft peaks form (the tips should curl over).

6. Beat in the vanilla seeds then remove bowl from the mixer.

7. Gently fold the flour mixture into the egg mixture.

8. Spoon onto an ungreased tube pan without creating large air bubbles.

9. Bake for 35-45 minutes or until golden brown.

10. Cool upside down for 1 hour then loosen sides using a thin knife and serve.

Chocolate Layer Cake

Makes 1 cake

Ingredients

½ cup unsalted butter, softened
1½ cups light brown sugar, packed
2 large eggs
2 teaspoons vanilla extract
½ cup good quality cocoa powder
2 teaspoons baking soda

1½ cups cake flour
⅔ cup sour cream
1 teaspoon instant coffee granules
⅔ cup water
Chocolate Ganache Icing (see page 139)

I love this recipe! The cake is very moist and full of chocolate flavor. It is also very versatile and perfect for cupcakes as well as elegant birthday cakes. For lazy days, I bake it in a 9x9-inch square pan and don't even frost it. This is the recipe I use for wedding cakes as well because it is easy to make and stays fresh for several days. Because this recipe uses cocoa powder, please see the source page in the back of the book to find high quality cocoa. It will make all the difference in the world.

1. Preheat oven to 350 degrees.

2. Butter and flour two 8-inch square pans; set aside.

3. In the bowl of a stand mixer fitted with the paddle attachment, combine butter and brown sugar.

4. Mix on medium speed for 5 minutes; scrape the bowl.

5. Add eggs and vanilla extract to the bowl and mix until combined; scrape the bowl.

6. Add remaining ingredients, except chocolate ganache icing, to the bowl and mix until smooth.

7. Divide the batter evenly between the cake pans.

8. Bake for 20-25 minutes; test for doneness using a toothpick.

9. Let cool for 10 minutes before unmolding.

10. Let cool completely before icing the cake with the Chocolate Ganache Icing.

Cookies & Bars

Chocolate Chip Cookies

Makes 8 servings

Ingredients

1 cup unsalted butter, softened
2 cups all purpose flour
1 teaspoon baking soda
1 teaspoon kosher salt
1 cup granulated sugar
½ cup light brown sugar, packed
2 teaspoons vanilla extract
2 large eggs
2 cups semi-sweet chocolate chips

1. Preheat oven to 325 degrees.

2. In a large bowl, cream butter on medium using a hand mixer.

3. While mixing, add the ingredients in the order listed above; mix well after each ingredient is added to achieve a smooth dough.

4. Line a cookie sheet with parchment paper.

5. Drop 2 tablespoons of dough about 2 inches apart across the cookie sheet.

6. Bake for 12-15 minutes or until golden brown; carefully rotate the cookie sheet halfway through the baking process.

7. Remove immediately.

Marian's Tip:
If you prefer chewy cookies, as soon as you remove the cookie sheet from the oven, grasp it with pot holders and rap the pan flat down on the counter twice. This will deflate the cookies slightly and greatly improve their chewy texture.

Royal Iced Sugar Cookies

Makes 24 cookies

Ingredients

1 cup (2 sticks) unsalted butter, softened
1½ cups granulated sugar
1 large egg
½ teaspoon pure vanilla extract
⅛ teaspoon butter-vanilla extract

1 teaspoon kosher salt
2½ cups all purpose flour
Royal Icing Glaze (see page 131)
Sprinkles
Colored Decorator Sugar (see page 140)

These are the best sugar cookies for decorating because they do not spread out too much in the oven. The chilling of the dough before baking really helps hold their shape as well. There is nothing worse than going to the trouble of rolling and cutting out cookies only to have them puff up and become all distorted in the oven. These behave beautifully and have a yummy, buttery taste that everyone loves. The finished cookies keep for 2 weeks if kept airtight, making them perfect for gift giving.

1. In the bowl of a stand mixer fitted with the beaters, combine the butter and sugar; mix on medium-high until the butter is fluffy.

2. Reduce the speed to low then add the egg, extracts, salt and flour; mix until a dough forms.

3. On a lightly floured surface, turn out the dough and divide it into 2 disks; cover in plastic wrap and chill for 1 hour.

4. On a lightly floured surface, roll out the dough until 1/4-inch thick; cut out cookies using floured cookie cutters.

5. Re-roll the dough scraps and continue cutting cookies.

6. Place the cookies on parchment-lined cookie sheets.

7. Chill the cookie sheets for 20 minutes.

8. Preheat oven to 350 degrees.

9. Bake cookies for 12-18 minutes or until pale golden.

10. Let cool completely then decorate with the Royal Icing Glaze and desired toppings.

Traditional Butter Cookies

Makes 60 cookies

Ingredients

¾ cup granulated sugar
1 cup unsalted butter, softened
1 large egg
1 teaspoon vanilla extract
¼ teaspoon pure almond extract
½ teaspoon butter-vanilla extract

½ teaspoon apple cider vinegar
½ teaspoon kosher salt
¼ teaspoon baking powder
2¼ cups unbleached all purpose flour
Powdered sugar

When I was 13 years old, I got a cookie press for my birthday. I remember racing to the kitchen to make cookies. I was watching as the dough magically extruded out of the cookie press onto the cookie sheets. Flowers, Christmas trees, camels and doggies all effortlessly done with the cookie press, ready for me to decorate with candy sprinkles. I was smitten. I had only known about drop cookies or the kind that had to be rolled out and cut using cookie cutters. This is the recipe that I liked best. I started adding the butter-vanilla extract to the recipe a few years ago just because I love it.

1. Preheat oven to 350 degrees.

2. In a bowl, combine sugar and butter; cream using an electric mixer for 1 minute or until uniformly blended.

3. Scrape the bowl then add the egg, vanilla, almond and butter-vanilla extracts.

4. Add remaining ingredients, except powdered sugar; mix on low speed until incorporated.

5. Fill the cookie press to the max line with dough; attach desired disk then press cookies onto ungreased cookie sheets (if you don't have a cookie press, roll the dough into 1-inch logs, chill then slice into 1/4-inch coins).

6. Bake for 10-15 minutes or until golden brown.

7. Top with powdered sugar while still warm and serve.

Marian's Tip:
To mix it up, add a few drops of food coloring to the mixture in step 4.

Gingersnap Cookies

Makes 84 cookies

Ingredients

¾ cup unsalted butter, softened
¾ cup dark brown sugar, packed
¾ cup molasses
2 teaspoons vanilla extract
1 large egg
½ teaspoon kosher salt
1 teaspoon baking soda

4 cups unbleached all purpose flour
1 tablespoon ground cinnamon
1 teaspoon ground cloves
2 teaspoons ground ginger
½ teaspoon ground nutmeg
1 teaspoon ground allspice

1. Preheat oven to 375 degrees.

2. Using an electric mixer, cream butter and sugar for 1 minute or until uniformly blended; scrape the bowl.

3. Add molasses, vanilla and egg; mix for an additional minute then scrape the bowl.

4. Add remaining ingredients and mix on low until the ingredients are incorporated.

5. Fill the cookie press to the max line with dough; attach desired disk then press cookies onto ungreased cookie sheets (if you don't have a cookie press, roll the dough into 1-inch logs, chill then slice into 1/4-inch coins).

6. Decorate as desired before or after baking.

7. Bake for 10-15 minutes or until golden brown.

8. Let cool before serving.

Marian's Tip:
Gingersnap dough is in the same family as Spritz Cookies, making it perfect for the cookie press.

Scottish Shortbread

Makes 12 cookies

Ingredients

1¼ cups (2½ sticks) unsalted butter, cold, cubed
3 tablespoons powdered sugar
¼ cup granulated sugar
2 tablespoons cornstarch
¼ cup cake flour
2 cups unbleached all purpose flour
The seeds from ½ of a split vanilla bean

This was my maternal grandmother's recipe and I have not found a finer one. She spent most of her years as a missionary in Bolivia. She was a tiny 4"10 mother of 11 children who lived into her late 90's. I spent the summer of 1980 with her and she pulled this recipe out of her bible and let me copy it down. I added the vanilla bean just because I love the flavor. These are perfectly sandy in texture, with the beautiful flavor from the butter. Each ingredient counts so make sure yours are fresh. These can also be stored airtight for up to 3 weeks.

1. Preheat oven to 275 degrees.

2. In the bowl of a stand mixer fitted with the paddles, combine all ingredients.

3. Blend on medium speed until the dough is uniform and no large pieces of butter are visible.

4. Pat the dough into a parchment-lined 8-inch square pan until 1/2-inch thick.

5. Using a knife, score the dough into finger-length rectangles by pressing the blade 1/8-inch deep into the dough.

6. Sprinkle additional granulated sugar over the dough.

7. Using a fork, press decorative marks all the way through the dough into each rectangle.

8. Bake for 1 hour or until a very pale blond color; let cool.

9. When almost cool, cut through the score marks using a serrated knife and serve.

Honey Tuile Cookies

Makes 100 cookies

Ingredients

½ cup unsalted butter, softened
2½ tablespoons honey
¾ cup all purpose flour, sifted

1 cup powdered sugar, sifted
2 large egg whites

1. Line a cookie sheet with a silicone-type aluminum foil.

2. In a bowl, combine butter and honey; mix on high using a hand mixer until fluffy.

3. Scrape the bowl and mix for an additional 30 seconds.

4. Add flour and sugar to the bowl; mix on low until incorporated then add the egg whites.

5. Stop to scrape the bowl then continue to blend until a uniform color is achieved; let rest for 30 minutes.

6. Preheat oven to 300 degrees.

7. Cut out a desired template using thin cardboard or plastic and place it on the cookie sheet.

8. Using a small spatula, spread a small amount of batter over the template.

9. Lift off the template (the cookies should remain on the cookie sheet).

10. Repeat until cookie sheet is filled.

11. Bake for 10 minutes or until brown (rotate the cookie sheet after 5 minutes to achieve even baking).

12. Let cool before serving.

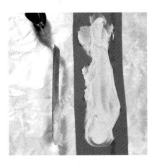

GO GATORS!

Happy Birthday

Oatmeal Cookies

Makes 36 cookies

Ingredients

1¾ cups unsalted butter, softened
1 cup granulated sugar
1 cup light brown sugar, packed
2 large eggs
1 teaspoon vanilla extract

½ teaspoon kosher salt
1¼ cups raisins
1 teaspoon baking soda
1½ cups all purpose flour
3 cups old fashioned rolled oats

Greg has a weakness for oatmeal cookies and he knows just how to sweet talk me into whipping up a batch. Whenever I mix the dough, he always asks if I can add lots of pecans. The happy compromise for me is to leave the pecans whole so I can just nibble around the nuts. This recipe has the perfect proportion of crispy edges and chewy centers. Be sure not to over-bake these or they get too crunchy.

1. Preheat oven to 350 degrees.

2. Line a cookie sheet with parchment paper.

3. In the bowl of a stand mixer fitted with the beaters, combine the butter and both sugars.

4. Beat on medium speed until fluffy then add the eggs, vanilla and salt.

5. Reduce the speed to low then add the remaining ingredients; mix until combined.

6. Using an ice cream scoop, place even scoops of batter, 2 inches apart, on the cookie sheet.

7. Bake for 12-15 minutes or until golden brown and slightly puffed.

8. Repeat with remaining dough and serve warm.

Marian's Tip:
These cookies can be stored in an airtight container
at room temperature for up to 3 days.

Peanut Butter & Jelly Cookies

Makes 48 small cookies

Ingredients

½ cup unsalted butter, softened
½ cup light brown sugar, packed
¼ cup granulated sugar
1 cup smooth peanut butter
1 large egg

½ teaspoon vanilla extract
1 cup all purpose flour
1 teaspoon baking soda
¼ teaspoon kosher salt
Jelly or ganache

These cookies are the peanuttiest cookies I have ever eaten. Once you have tried these, you will never crave another peanut butter cookie. They are sandy, tender and irresistible. You can shape them the traditional way or make little thumbprints and fill the centers. Chocolate filling is nice but my homemade strawberry jelly is my very favorite. Please note that this dough is best made ahead of time and kept chilled. The good news is that it will keep in the refrigerator for a week or in the freezer for a month, so you can have fresh cookies any time.

1. In a bowl, combine butter, sugars and peanut butter; mix well using a hand mixer until smooth and creamy.

2. Add egg and vanilla to the bowl; mix well.

3. Scrape the sides of the bowl and sift the flour, baking soda and salt over the batter; mix until a smooth dough forms then cover and chill for 2 hours.

4. Preheat oven to 325 degrees.

5. Using a spoon, scoop out chunks the size of large grapes, roll them into balls and place them on a parchment-lined cookie sheet.

6. Using your pinky finger, make an indentation into the center of each ball and top with additional sugar.

7. Bake on the center rack in the oven for 10 minutes then carefully rotate the cookie sheet.

8. Carefully press the centers of each cookie using a spoon and bake for an additional 10 minutes.

9. Let cool, fill the centers with jelly or ganache and serve.

Cactus Pear Jam

Gluten-Free Peanut Butter Cookies

Makes 18 cookies

Ingredients

2 cups smooth peanut butter
2 cups granulated sugar
¼ teaspoon kosher salt
1 teaspoon baking soda
2 large eggs
2 tablespoons cornstarch
2 teaspoons vanilla extract

I have never seen a recipe for peanut butter cookies that called for so little starch or flour. I think that is what keeps these little gems so peanutty. I love testing gluten free recipes and have learned to only accept them into my repertoire if they are good enough to serve to everyone.

Marian's Tip: These cookies will keep at room temperature for up to 3 days.

1. In a bowl, combine all ingredients.

2. Mix using a hand mixer until well combined.

3. Divide dough and form it into 18 balls.

4. Place the balls onto parchment-lined cookie sheets.

5. Pat down the top of each ball with your palm.

6. Sprinkle tops with additional sugar.

7. Press the tines of a fork twice onto each dough ball and scrape to form a criss cross pattern.

8. Preheat oven to 325 degrees.

9. Bake for 12-18 minutes or until slightly puffed and brown.

10. Serve warm.

Grandma's Classic Spritz Cookies

Makes 72 cookies

Ingredients

1 cup unsalted butter, softened
½ cup granulated sugar
1 large egg
1 teaspoon vanilla extract
¼ teaspoon butter-vanilla extract
½ teaspoon kosher salt
2½ cups unbleached all purpose flour

This was my paternal grandmother's recipe. I was lucky to have inherited her old metal red and white checkered recipe file. I can tell by the oil stains, blobs of food coloring and her notes in the margins on the faded recipe card that this was a Christmas favorite of hers. Though I never got to bake by her side, I still make these cookies each year. Like so many of us, this is the connection with the past and family rituals that make the whole baking experience so enjoyable. I am told by my dad that I have my grandma's energy and feisty disposition. I take that as a compliment.

1. Preheat oven to 375 degrees.

2. In the bowl of an electric mixer, combine the butter and sugar; mix on low speed for 1 minute then scrape the bowl.

3. Add the egg and vanilla to the bowl; mix for 1 additional minute then scrape the bowl.

4. Add remaining ingredients to the bowl; mix on low speed until the flour is incorporated.

5. Fill the cookie press to the max line with dough; attach desired disk then press cookies onto ungreased cookie sheets (if you don't have a cookie press, roll the dough into 1-inch logs, chill then slice into 1/4-inch coins).

6. Bake for 8-10 minutes or until golden brown.

7. Serve warm.

Lemon Spritz Cookies

Makes 60 cookies

Dough Ingredients

1 cup unsalted butter, softened
½ cup granulated sugar
1 large egg
1 teaspoon vanilla extract
¼ teaspoon butter vanilla extract
½ teaspoon kosher salt
2½ cups unbleached all purpose flour

Lemon Glaze

1 cup powdered sugar
3 tablespoons fresh lemon juice
2 teaspoons lemon zest

Did you ever accidentally add salt to a recipe instead of sugar? I think every baker does this at least once and it happened to me with this recipe. I am the type of person who likes cookie dough as much as the cookies themselves, so I realized that I made this awful-tasting mistake before baking them. Being a mischievous child, I went to my siblings holding the bowl of dough and told them how delicious it was. I convinced them to have a taste. I don't remember how they got back at me but I am sure they did. When made correctly, these cookies are irresistible.

1. Preheat oven to 350 degrees.

2. In a bowl, combine the dough ingredients in the order listed above; mix using a hand mixer until a smooth dough forms.

3. Fill the cookie press to the max line with dough; attach a disk with the larger holes then press cookies onto ungreased cookie sheets (if you don't have a cookie press, roll the dough into 1-inch logs, chill then slice them into 1/4-inch coins).

4. Bake for 8-10 minutes or until golden brown.

5. To make the glaze, combine all glaze ingredients in a bowl; mix well.

6. Top each cookie with glaze while still warm.

Marian's Tip:
To turn these into lime cookies, substitute lime for the lemon juice and zest in the glaze then add a couple of drops of green food coloring.

Coconut Snowflake Cookies

Makes 72 cookies

Ingredients

½ cup solid white shortening
½ cup unsalted butter, softened
4 tablespoons cream cheese, softened
1 cup granulated sugar
1 large egg
2 teaspoons coconut extract
1 teaspoon butter-vanilla extract
¼ teaspoon baking soda
1 teaspoon kosher salt
2¼ cups unbleached all purpose flour
½ cup sweetened and shredded coconut flakes

My friend Marla Drumright in Ottawa, Kansas gave me this recipe in 1985. Of all my friends, she is the one who has "mothered" me the most over the years. She was always dispensing advice on how to raise kids, grow tomatoes, sew a quilt and live a great life. She is also a great cook and baker. Marla starts her holiday cookie baking in November and does not stop until her freezer is full. The cream cheese is the secret to this delectable cookie.

1. Preheat oven to 375 degrees.

2. Place all ingredients, except coconut flakes, in the order listed above into the food processor.

3. Secure the lid then pulse and blend until a soft dough forms.

4. Fill the cookie press to the max line with dough; attach a disk with the larger holes then press cookies onto ungreased cookie sheets (if you don't have a cookie press, roll the dough into 1-inch logs, chill then slice them into 1/4-inch coins).

5. Top cookies with coconut flakes.

6. Bake for 10-15 minutes or until golden brown.

7. Serve warm.

Rugelach

Makes 32 cookies

Ingredients

Vienna Pastry Pie Crust, unbaked (see page 67)
½ cup apricot jam
½ cup granulated sugar
1 tablespoon ground cinnamon

½ cup raisins
½ cup chopped walnuts or pecans, toasted
3 tablespoons unsalted butter, melted
⅓ cup cinnamon sugar

1. Line 2 sheet pans with parchment paper; set aside.

2. Divide the dough from the Vienna Pastry Pie Crust into 2 flat balls.

3. On a floured surface, roll each ball out into a large 1/4-inch thick circle.

4. Divide jam between the circles and spread evenly.

5. Divide sugar, cinnamon, raisins and nuts between the circles.

6. Using a pizza wheel, cut circles into 16 equal wedges.

7. Starting at the wider end, roll up each wedge then tuck the ends under.

8. Place rolls on the sheet pans and place the pans in the refrigerator.

9. Chill while preheating the oven to 375 degrees.

10. Right before baking, brush the rolls with butter and top with cinnamon sugar.

11. Bake for 20 minutes or until well browned (it is normal for some of the filling to leak out of the cookies during baking).

12. Peel the cookies off the parchment paper while still hot and serve.

Marian's Tip:
If you like chocolate rugelach, omit the apricot jam, raisins and nuts.
Just add ½ cup of Nutella and a cup of semi-sweet mini chocolate chips.

Cinnamon Biscotti

Makes 40 Biscotti

Ingredients

1 cup + 1 tablespoon granulated sugar

5 ounces unsalted butter, melted

2 large eggs

2 teaspoons vanilla extract

½ teaspoon kosher salt

2 tablespoons ground cinnamon

1½ teaspoons baking powder

2 cups all purpose flour, sifted

Topping

½ cup granulated sugar

1 tablespoon ground cinnamon

One year, when biscotti became a popular coffee snack in America, I was determined to come up with some amazing homemade biscotti that I could "wow" Wolfgang with. He loves a good espresso with biscotti. Well, I "invented" 50 different biscotti recipes out of which this recipe as well as a coconut biscotti recipe were the only winners. When I told Wolf about all of my failed biscotti attempts leading me to come up with the two "keepers", he just smiled and reminded me that creating recipes is a little like eating artichokes; you go through so much to get so little.

1. Preheat oven to 325 degrees.

2. Line 2 cookie sheets with parchment paper.

3. In a large bowl, combine all ingredients; mix well using a spoon until a uniform dough forms.

4. Transfer dough to a gallon-size plastic zipper bag and snip a 1½-inch hole across 1 corner of the bag.

5. Pipe 2 logs per cookie sheet (2 inches wide) across the length of the cookie sheet.

6. Sprinkle logs with topping ingredients.

7. Bake the logs for 20-30 minutes or until puffed and edges are beginning to brown.

8. Remove from oven, lower the oven temperature to 200 degrees and let cool for 5 minutes.

9. Cut the logs across to form biscotti fingers, spread them out on the cookie sheet so they do not touch and bake for an additional 20-30 minutes or until crispy.

Lively Lemon Bars

Makes 18 bars

Crust Ingredients

1½ cups all purpose flour
1 tablespoon lemon zest
¼ cup powdered sugar
½ cup unsalted butter, melted

Lemon Filling:

4 large eggs
1¼ cups granulated sugar
2 tablespoons all purpose flour
½ cup fresh lemon juice
2 tablespoons lemon zest
½ teaspoon kosher salt
½ teaspoon pure vanilla extract

The first time I met Wolf was at his café in Orlando. It was an early morning and he was scheduled to appear as a guest on a local radio spot. I was busy prepping all the desserts for the day, when all of a sudden I heard that unmistakable Austrian voice say: "Hello, leesten, do we have somesing sweet to eat or what?" I just happened to have made these bars and that is when I discovered how much Wolf adores lemons. He kept eating them, one after another, then breaking off more bits to nibble on as he chatted. When he was leaving, he asked me to pack him a box of the lemon bars to take home. He gave me two kisses, said "sank-you princess" and winked as he walked out with the box tucked under his arm.

1. Preheat oven to 350 degrees.

2. In a bowl, combine all crust ingredients; mix using a fork until a crumbly dough forms.

3. Press the dough into the bottom of a greased 9x9-inch baking pan.

4. Bake for 15-20 minutes or until a very light golden brown color is achieved.

5. In a bowl, combine all filling ingredients; whisk well until smooth.

6. Pour filling over the hot crust.

7. Place the pan back in the oven and bake for an additional 20-25 minutes or until the filling sets.

8. Let cool completely, cut into 18 thin bars and serve.

Marian's Tip:
You can turn these into lime or grapefruit bars by substituting the juice and zest.

Date Bars

Makes 24 bars

Ingredients

1 cup pitted dates, finely chopped
½ cup water
¼ cup granulated sugar
2 teaspoons vanilla extract
½ cup light brown sugar, packed

1 cup old fashioned rolled oats
½ cup all purpose flour
½ teaspoon baking soda
½ teaspoon kosher salt
½ cup unsalted butter, melted

Of all the bar-type cookies, these have always been my favorite. I am a sucker for any type of oatmeal streusel topping. The thick date filling nestled in between the brown crust and the topping are just about the best sweet snack treat I can think of. This recipe, being quite easy to make, was one of the first sweets my mom allowed me to bake all by myself.

1. Preheat oven to 350 degrees.

2. Butter a 8x8-inch baking pan; set aside.

3. In a microwave-safe bowl, combine the dates, water and sugar.

4. Microwave until the mixture comes to a boil; stir then microwave for an additional minute.

5. Let cool then stir in the vanilla; set aside.

6. In a bowl, combine remaining ingredients; stir using a fork until crumbly and uniform in color.

7. Press half of the oat mixture into the pan.

8. Spread the date filling over the oat mixture in the pan then top with remaining oat mixture.

9. Bake for 25-30 minutes or until golden brown.

10. Let cool, cut into bars and serve.

Chocolate Truffle Bars

Makes 15 bars

Crust Ingredients

1½ cups almonds, toasted and ground
1 cup powdered sugar
½ cup all purpose flour
½ cup unsalted butter, melted

Filling

1¼ cups unsalted butter
2 cups semi-sweet chocolate chips
8 large eggs
1 cup granulated sugar
¼ cup all purpose flour

Icing

1½ cups almonds, toasted and ground
2 cups powdered sugar
¼ teaspoon almond extract
¼ teaspoon butter vanilla extract
¼ teaspoon kosher salt
1 cup unsalted butter, softened
3 large egg whites

1. Grease a 1/4 sheet pan and set aside.

2. In a bowl, combine all crust ingredients; press into the bottom of the sheet pan.

3. In a microwave-safe bowl, combine butter and chocolate chips; microwave for 2 minutes or until chocolate is melted.

4. In the bowl of a stand mixer fitted with the whip attachment, combine the eggs and sugar; whip on highest speed for 5 minutes or until fluffy and pale yellow.

5. Fold in the flour then add the chocolate mixture and mix until combined.

6. Preheat oven to 325 degrees.

7. Pour the batter into the sheet pan and bake for 30-35 minutes or until top is dry and cracked; let cool completely.

8. In the bowl of a stand mixer fitted with the beater attachment, combine all icing ingredients; beat on high for 5 minutes or until fluffy then scrape the bowl and mix for 1 additional minute.

9. Spread the icing over the top of the batter, cut into bars and serve.

Pies & Such

Vienna Pastry Pie Crust

Makes one 8-inch crust

Ingredients

1 cup unsalted butter, cold and cubed

1 package (8 ounces) cream cheese

½ teaspoon kosher salt

2 cups all purpose flour

Vienna pastry is perfect for pie crusts. The beauty of this recipe is that it can be made by hand, in a mixer or even a food processor. The cream cheese in this recipe keeps the dough nice and tender. You can treat it much more roughly than standard pie dough and it will stay tender. It is a dream to work with as it does not get sticky. It bakes up flaky and tender, perfect for cookies and tarts. It is also the dough used for making rugelach (see page 59), a rolled and filled Hanukkah pastry that is fantastic. Once you make this dough, you will see why I am so crazy about it.

1. In a food processor or a stand mixer, combine all ingredients; process until a dough ball forms.

2. Shape the dough into 2 flat and round disks, reserving 1 disk for future use.

3. Cover and refrigerate for 1 hour.

4. Preheat oven to 350 degrees.

5. On a lightly floured surface, roll out the dough and shape it to fit a pie pan.

6. Gently fit the dough into the pie pan without stretching.

7. Crimp the edges then cover the crust with parchment paper.

8. Take a cheesecloth bag filled with dry beans (see tools on page 9) and place the bag onto the parchment-lined pie crust.

9. Bake for 25 minutes, remove the cheesecloth bag then bake for an additional 5 minutes.

10. Remove and fill crust as desired.

Banana Cream Pie

Makes 1 pie

Ingredients

2 cups heavy whipping cream, cold
⅓ cup powdered sugar
2 teaspoons pure vanilla extract
½ cup Banana Jam (see page 140)

Vienna Pastry Pie Crust (see page 67)
5 ripe bananas, sliced
Pastry Cream, cooled (see page 125)

In Africa, one fruit we never had a shortage of was the banana. My mom was always sneaking extra bananas into our foods and added even more into recipes that already called for them. Fortunately for this pie, it makes for an extraordinarily delightful banana experience. The first time I made this for Greg in my college dorm kitchenette, we ate it right out of the tin with plastic forks. After a few bites, Greg just smiled and said "will you marry me?"

1. In a bowl, combine cream, sugar and vanilla.

2. Using a hand mixer, beat until stiff peaks form; set aside.

3. Spread the banana jam over the bottom of the prepared Vienna Pastry Pie Crust.

4. Fold the banana slices into the pastry cream, reserving some banana slices for garnishing.

5. Spread the pastry cream into the pie crust.

6. Top with vanilla cream mixture and create decorative swirls using a teaspoon.

7. Top with remaining banana slices.

8. Serve immediately.

Key Lime Meringue Pie

Makes 1 pie

Ingredients

Vienna Pastry pie crust, unbaked (see page 67)
1 can (14 ounces) sweetened condensed milk
4 large egg yolks

1 tablespoon fresh lime zest
½ cup fresh lime juice
Swiss Meringue (see page 132)

Before the 1920s, the Florida Keys used to have plentiful amounts of tiny, piquant Key Limes. Hurricanes have since all but destroyed them. Today, virtually all of the Key Limes in our markets come from Mexico. No matter if this pie is made with Key Limes or the more familiar Persian variety, it is still delicious. A perfect marriage of sweet and tart. Many argue about the right topping for this pie. Some claim that meringue is the authentic topping and others claim that whipped cream is. Considering its Florida Keys origin and the use of canned sweetened condensed milk due to a lack of refrigeration in the Keys, the meringue topping seems more logical to me.

1. Preheat oven to 350 degrees.

2. In a large bowl, combine milk, eggs, lime zest and juice.

3. Using a hand mixer, mix until smooth.

4. Pour mixture into the prepared but unbaked Vienna Pastry Pie Crust.

5. Bake for 20 minutes or until the custard sets.

6. Prepare Swiss Meringue and pile on top of the pie into decorative swirls.

7. Preheat oven to 500 degrees.

8. Bake pie for 5 minutes or until edges are browned.

9. Serve each piece of pie with a lime wedge and topped with additional lime zest.

Marian's Tip:
You can use a blow torch to achieve even faster browning.

Buttermilk Pie

Makes 1 pie

Ingredients

1¼ cups granulated sugar
⅔ cup light brown sugar, packed
½ cup unsalted butter, melted
1 teaspoon pure vanilla extract
¼ cup buttermilk

⅔ cup heavy whipping cream
8 large egg yolks
Vienna Pastry Pie Crust, unbaked (see page 67)
Powdered sugar

For me, this pie is the most beguiling of all the Southern pies. The ingredients are so plain in taste on their own but are transformed into creamy and caramely tasting custard in the oven. It is quite unlike anything I have ever tasted before. It is decadent, rich yet sweet and mild. Completely addictive. For lazy days, I use store bought frozen puff pastries in place of the homemade Vienna Pastry Pie Crust.

1. Preheat oven to 325 degrees.

2. In a bowl, combine all ingredients, except pie crust and powdered sugar; whisk well until smooth.

3. Pour mixture into the prepared but unbaked Vienna Pastry Pie Crust.

4. Bake for 15 minutes.

5. Lower the temperature to 300 degrees and bake for an additional 40 minutes or until set.

6. Let cool.

7. Dust with powdered sugar and serve at room temperature.

Raspberry Chiffon Pie

Makes 1 pie

Ingredients

2 cups fresh raspberries

1 pouch (3 ounces) liquid fruit pectin

1½ cups granulated sugar

Vienna Pastry Pie Crust (see page 67)

2 envelopes (¼ ounce each) unflavored gelatin

½ cup water

3 ounces cream cheese, warmed

½ cup frozen raspberries, thawed

2½ cups heavy whipping cream

1 cup powdered sugar

1. In a saucepan, combine fresh raspberries, pectin and sugar.

2. Boil for 5 minutes, let it cool then pour it into the prepared and cooled pie crust.

3. In a bowl, combine gelatin and water; let stand for 5 minutes.

4. Heat the bowl in the microwave until hot and all of the gelatin has dissolved.

5. Whisk in the cream cheese until smooth.

6. Stir in the thawed raspberries.

7. In a separate bowl, combine remaining ingredients.

8. Using a hand mixer fitted with the whisk, beat the cream until stiff peaks form.

9. Fold 1/3 of the whipped cream into the gelatin mixture and spread it over the prepared Vienna Pastry Pie Crust.

10. Top with remaining whipped cream, creating decorative swirls using the back of a teaspoon.

11. Chill for 3 hours before serving.

Pavlova

Makes 6 mounds

Ingredients
Swiss Meringue (see page 132)
Powdered sugar for dusting
1½ cups heavy whipping cream
4½ tablespoons powdered sugar
½ cup Passion Fruit Curd (see Marian's Tip in the Lemon Curd recipe on page 133)
2 cups assorted berries, such as raspberries, blueberries, kiwi, currants, blackberries

Pavlova is a meringue and fruit dessert that hails from Australia and is named after Anna Pavlova, the famous Russian ballerina. It is usually served with whipped cream and passion fruit. Here, I pair it with delightful passion fruit curd. The contrast between the crispy meringue, lightly whipped cream and tangy passion fruit is a true flavor and texture explosion. The meringue keeps well if sealed against humidity, making this a great dessert to prepare in advance.

1. Preheat oven to 200 degrees.

2. Using a large spoon, scoop 6 mounds of meringue, about 3 1/2 inches in diameter, onto a parchment-lined baking sheet.

3. Using the back of the spoon, form a well in the center of each mound.

4. Lightly dust mounds with powdered sugar.

5. Bake for 90 minutes or until dry to the touch but still white in color; let cool completely.

6. When ready to serve, combine whipping cream with powdered sugar in a medium bowl and mix using a hand mixer until stiff peaks form.

7. Place a dollop of whipped cream onto each meringue.

8. Top with a spoon of passion fruit curd and garnish with berries.

Alice Jo's Rhubarb Crisp

Ingredients

4 cups rhubarb, chopped
1½ cups granulated sugar, divided
6 slices day-old bread, crusts removed and cubed
½ cup unsalted butter, melted

The taste of rhubarb is one that Greg and I can't get enough of. When I look through my recipe file, I am amazed at how many rhubarb recipes I have. This one is from Alice Jo at the First Baptist Church in Ottawa, Kansas. She used to make it in a big 9x13-inch dish to bring to Pot Luck dinners at the church. Whenever Greg would see her place this dish on the dessert table, he made a bee-line to it as soon as the blessing ended.

1. In a bowl, combine rhubarb and 3/4 cup sugar; toss and let rest for 15 minutes.

2. In a separate bowl, combine bread cubes, butter and remaining sugar; toss well.

3. Grease 6 ramekins and place them on a cookie sheet.

4. Divide rhubarb mixture evenly between the ramekins.

5. Top each ramekin evenly with the bread mixture.

6. Preheat oven to 350 degrees.

7. Bake for 35-45 minutes or until brown and bubbly.

8. Serve plain or topped with softly whipped cream.

Wolfgang's Apple Strudel

Makes 1 large strudel

Ingredients

2½ cups unbleached all purpose flour

¼ teaspoon kosher salt

1 cup water, room temperature

¼ cup vegetable oil

1 teaspoon red wine vinegar

Apple Strudel Filling (see page 138)

1½ cups unsalted butter, melted

½ cup unflavored breadcrumbs, finely ground

This is the strudel Wolf taught me to make. I fell in love with baking all over again the first time I made it. This recipe is one of the reasons I still thank God every day for making me a pastry chef. This strudel is all about the dough. I love stretching it as it is smooth like velvet and impossibly thin.

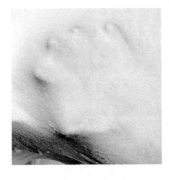

1. In the bowl of a stand mixer fitted with the dough hooks, combine all ingredients, except Apple Strudel Filling, butter and breadcrumbs.

2. Mix on low then medium for 30 seconds; scrape the bowl then continue mixing for 7 minutes or until the dough is very wet and sticky.

3. Place a large square of plastic wrap on the counter; apply oil using your fingers.

4. Transfer the dough to the oiled plastic wrap and pat it into an even ball.

5. Wrap the dough ball in the plastic wrap and let it rest on the counter for 1 hour.

6. Spread out an old tablecloth on the table and lightly sprinkle it with flour, adding some extra flour to the center of the tablecloth.

7. Unwrap and place the dough ball in the center of the tablecloth, flour the top then roll the dough into a large circle using a rolling pin.

8. Flour your hands and slip them under the dough with your palms down.

9. Make loose fists and gently pull dough toward you. Repeat a few times by moving hands a few inches and pulling again to thin out the dough. If the dough gets to shiny or sticky, flour it. Pinch together any tears. Stretch the edges by pulling dough over the edge of the table until the dough hangs like a tablecloth.

10. Place a piece of paper with writing under the dough, if you can see the print through the dough, it is thin enough. Trim off the thicker edge of the dough using scissors and discard.

11. Preheat oven to 350 degrees and grease a large, rimmed baking pan.

12. Brush dough with butter then top with breadcrumbs.

13. Place the strudel filling in a long, fat row along the short side of the dough. Use the tablecloth to reach under the dough, flip it over the apples and roll it into a log. Place the baking pan next to the strudel and flip it into the pan using the same tablecloth method. Pull the ends and tuck them under the strudel. Brush strudel with additional butter and bake for 1 hour or until dark brown.

14. Dust with powdered sugar, slice into wedges and serve.

Apple Confit Torte

Makes 1 torte

Ingredients

12 Granny Smith apples, peeled, cored and sliced ⅛-inch thick
⅓ cup fresh lemon juice
1 cup granulated sugar

In French, the word "confit" refers to a dish made by gently cooking a goose or duck in its own fat. Nowadays, the term is used to describe many foods that are cooked in their own juices. This recipe uses only 3 simple ingredients, yet the cake is exquisite looking and has a beautiful texture from all the layers of apple slices. The taste? Pure apple goodness on a whole other level. This dessert is truly more than the sum of its parts. Don't be afraid as you try to stack so many apple slices into the pan. They will all melt down into thin layers to form a solid cake of apples. Slow, gentle baking is the secret to this dessert. I recommend using a mandolin for easy slicing.

1. Butter a 8-inch round pan with 4-inch tall sides.

2. Evenly layer a double row of apples in the pan, pressing the apples against the pan's edge.

3. Sprinkle some lemon juice and sugar over the apples.

4. Repeat this process until all the apple slices are layered and stacked up higher than the pan's sides.

5. Cover the top with a piece of buttered parchment paper as well as aluminum foil.

6. Place the pan inside a larger pan holding 1-inch of hot water and transfer it to the cold oven.

7. Set oven to 275 degrees.

8. Bake for 3 hours.

9. Remove and let cool.

10. Cut into wedges and serve.

Marian's Tip:
Serve this with sweetened whipped cream.

Lemon Tart with Melon Ribbons

Makes 1 tart

Ingredients

Vienna Pastry Pie Crust, unbaked (see page 67)

Lemon Curd (see page 133)

¼ of a cantaloupe, peeled and seeded

¼ of a honeydew melon, peeled and seeded

When I first made this for Wolf at the restaurant, I could barely get the lemon curd into the tart because he kept tasting the curd right out of the bowl. He is crazy about any dessert made with lemon. When I had finished it, he picked up a fork and ate half of it before I could cut it and put it on a dessert plate. I did not mind because I consider it to be an honor when Wolf likes my desserts. Besides, he is really fun to feed!

1. Preheat oven to 350 degrees.

2. Grease a fluted tart pan.

3. On a lightly floured surface, roll out the dough from the Vienna Pastry Pie Crust until 1/8-inch thick.

4. Roll dough up on a rolling pin and lift it over the tart pan then unroll the dough and let it ease onto the bottom of the tart pan without stretching.

5. Press dough evenly up the sides of the pan.

6. Use the rolling pin to trim the excess dough by rolling it over the pan's edges.

7. Use a cheesecloth bag filled with dry beans (see tools on page 9) to weigh the pastry down.

8. Bake for 25-30 minutes or until edges are brown.

9. Remove the cheesecloth bag and bake for an additional 5 minutes; remove and let cool.

10. Fill the tart with lemon curd until 1/4 inch below the tart's top. Use a mandolin to slice long and thin ribbons from the cantaloupe and honeydew melon.

11. Roll each ribbon into a coil, arrange on top of the lemon curd and serve immediately.

Greg's Peach Cobbler

Makes 1 cobbler

Biscuit Ingredients

1½ cups all purpose flour
⅓ cup granulated sugar
½ teaspoon kosher salt
2½ teaspoons baking powder
½ cup unsalted butter, cold and cubed
½ cup sour cream

Fruit Filling Ingredients

6-8 peaches, ripe and very fragrant, sliced
¼ cup quick-cook tapioca
1 cup granulated sugar
¼ teaspoon citric acid

Peaches are Greg's favorite fruit. When the produce section at our local market starts to smell of sweet peaches in the summer time, Greg starts dreaming about a cobbler. He likes it best with a biscuit topping and prefers tapioca as a thickener for the fruit because it is the most clear. His favorite part is when the fruit juices bubble up the sides of the pan in the oven and start to caramelize. This warm cobbler with softly whipped cream on the side is sure to make my dear husband grin from ear to ear.

1. Butter an 8x8-inch pan; set aside.

2. Fit the food processor with the metal S blade.

3. Add all biscuit ingredients to the food processor.

4. Secure the lid and pulse until a dough ball forms.

5. On a lightly floured surface, pat out the dough into a rectangle.

6. Fold dough into thirds like a business letter and pat it back out into a rectangle; repeat.

7. Cut dough into twelve 2-inch squares and pat remaining scraps into the pan to cover the bottom.

8. In a bowl, combine all fruit filling ingredients and spoon it into the pan; arrange biscuit squares on top then sprinkle with additional sugar.

9. Preheat oven to 400 degrees.

10. Bake for 15 minutes then lower the temperature to 350 degrees and bake for an additional 45 minutes or until fruit filling is very bubbly and biscuits are brown; serve warm.

Crackers,
Breads & Pizzas

Amish Crispy Crackers

Makes 24 crackers

Cracker Ingredients

3½ cups unbleached all purpose flour
2 tablespoons granulated sugar
½ teaspoon baking powder
1 tablespoon kosher salt

1 teaspoon baker's ammonia (see source page)
½ cup unsalted butter, cold and cubed
1¼ cups buttermilk

Toppings:

Sesame seeds	Curry powder	Onion powder	Parmesan cheese
Poppy seeds	Chili powder	Dehydrated onions	Cinnamon sugar
Caraway seeds	Granulated sugar	Chili flakes	Kosher salt

1. Fit a food processor with the metal S blade.

2. Place all cracker ingredients, except buttermilk, into the food processor.

3. While processing, pour the buttermilk through the feed tube; process until a dough ball forms then refrigerate the dough for at least 1 hour.

4. Preheat oven to 400 degrees.

5. Divide the dough in half and keep one half refrigerated.

6. On a lightly floured surface, roll out the dough until 1/16-inch thick.

7. Brush water over the dough using a pastry brush then top with desired toppings and some kosher salt.

8. Place the dough onto a parchment-lined cookie sheet then prick the dough all over with a fork.

9. Cut dough into desired shapes then bake for 10-20 minutes or until brown.

10. Remove and repeat with remaining dough.

Southern Cheese Straws

Makes 48 crackers

Ingredients

1⅔ cups unbleached all purpose flour
2 tablespoons dry mustard powder
2 teaspoons cayenne pepper
½ teaspoon ground turmeric
2 teaspoons kosher salt
1 large egg
½ cup unsalted butter, softened
6 ounces extra sharp cheddar cheese, shredded
2 ounces blue cheese, crumbled

The first time I made these crackers was in my college dorm kitchenette. I found the recipe in a magazine and since it said "Southern" in the recipe title, I was sure Greg would love them. I borrowed a friend's bicycle and rode to the local grocery store to buy the ingredients. My kitchen tools at the time were pitiful and of the cheapest quality. When I was stirring the dough, my metal spoon bent almost in half. I then used my best tools, my hands to finish mixing the dough.

1. Preheat oven to 400 degrees.

2. Place all ingredients into the food processor.

3. Pulse until a dough ball forms then process for 30 seconds or until the dough is uniformly smooth without any visible cheese pieces.

4. Fill the cookie press to the max line with dough then attach a disk with large holes (if you don't have a cookie press, roll the dough into 1-inch logs, chill then slice into 1/4-inch coins).

5. Press crackers onto ungreased cookie sheets.

6. Sprinkle additional kosher salt over the crackers.

7. Bake for 15-20 minutes or until deep brown and crispy.

8. Remove and serve.

Breton Butter Bread

Makes 1 round loaf

Ingredients

1 cup water, room temperature
1 envelope (2½ teaspoons) dry active yeast
2¼ cups all purpose flour

½ teaspoon kosher salt
¾ cup unsalted butter, softened
½ cup granulated sugar

The real name for this sweet is Kouign Amann (Qeen-ah-man) which means "bread and butter" in the local tongue of Brittany, France. It is the simplest of yeast bread dough, rolled and folded around layers of butter and sugar. It is flaky and puffed like a croissant yet sweet and caramelized at the same time. Just heavenly!

1. In the bowl of a stand mixer fitted with the dough hook, combine water, yeast, flour and salt.

2. Mix on medium speed for 7 minutes; stop to scrape the bowl after 3 minutes.

3. Remove the dough and place it in an oiled, gallon-size zipper bag; chill for 2 hours.

4. On a lightly floured surface, roll out the dough into a 8x12-inch rectangle.

5. Dot the top of the dough with butter then top it with sugar.

6. Fold dough into thirds like a business letter then roll it out again into a 8x12-inch rectangle; let it rest for 20 minutes.

7. Repeat step 6 two additional times.

8. Preheat oven to 400 degrees.

9. Place the dough into a 8-inch round ungreased pan; press corners to fit then let it rest for 30 minutes.

10. Bake for 20 minutes, baste the top of the dough with the butter that has surfaced then continue to bake for 25 minutes or until dark brown; let cool before slicing.

Cast Iron Dutch Oven Sourdough Bread

Makes 1 loaf

Ingredients

3 cups all purpose flour
¼ teaspoon active dry yeast
1 tablespoon kosher salt

7 ounces water
3 ounces beer (lager type)
1 tablespoon white vinegar

1. In a bowl, combine all ingredients; stir using a spoon for 30 seconds.

2. Cover the bowl with plastic wrap and let it rest on the counter for 8-18 hours to ferment.

3. Line a bowl similar in size to your dutch oven with parchment paper and apply non-stick spray.

4. On a lightly floured surface, quickly shape the dough into a ball using floured hands.

5. Transfer the dough to the parchment-lined bowl; let rise for 2 hours.

6. After 90 minutes of the rising process, place the empty cast iron dutch oven with the lid in the oven at 450 degrees to preheat.

7. Once the 2 hours of rising is complete, sprinkle a layer of flour over the dough and slash the top with a sharp knife to make a decorative line.

8. Open the oven and carefully remove the lid of the dutch oven using an oven mitt.

9. Pick up the dough by the parchment paper and quickly lower it into the dutch oven with the parchment paper; cover with the lid and close the oven.

10. Reduce the heat to 425 degrees and bake for 30 minutes.

11. Remove the lid of the dutch oven and continue to bake for 30 minutes or until dark brown and internal loaf temperature is 200 degrees; let cool before serving.

Basic Focaccia Bread

Makes 1 loaf

Sponge Ingredients

¼ cup water, room temperature
1 package dry active yeast
1 tablespoon honey
½ cup bread flour

For the Pan

¼ cup extra-virgin olive oil, divided

Dough Ingredients

2 cups bread flour
1 teaspoon kosher salt
⅓ cup olive oil
1 cup water, room temperature

Topping

Blue Cheese & Grape Topping
(see page 139)

1. In the bowl of a stand mixer fitted with the hook attachment, add all sponge ingredients; mix on low until a thin batter is achieved.

2. Add the flour and salt from the dough ingredients to the bowl; let rest for 20 minutes.

3. Pour oil and water over the flour and turn the mixer on low then medium speed.

4. Mix for 7 minutes on medium speed until the dough is very wet; stop to scrape the bowl after 3 minutes.

5. Pour half of the olive oil into a 1/4 sheet pan and swirl it around the pan.

6. Transfer the dough onto the pan then top the dough with remaining olive oil.

7. Pat and pull dough to fit the shape of the pan; let rest for 30 minutes.

8. Preheat oven to 400 degrees.

9. Dimple the dough all over with the tip of your finger; let rest for 5 minutes.

10. Add the toppings then bake for 20-25 minutes or until brown and puffed.

11. Cut bread into squares and serve hot.

Sour Cream Dinner Rolls

Makes 24 rolls

Ingredients

1 cup (8 ounces) sour cream
½ cup unsalted butter, melted then cooled
½ cup granulated sugar
2½ teaspoons kosher salt

2 packages active dry yeast
½ cup water
2 large eggs
4 cups unbleached all purpose flour

My friend Marla gave me this simple recipe. She claims that it is of Hungarian origin. Even though there is ample sour cream in the dough, it is traditional to eat the rolls slathered with more sour cream instead of butter. It sounds odd until you try it. The sour cream in this recipe makes rolls that are sublimely light and soft with a wonderful moistness and tang. The dough keeps for a day or two in the fridge and even freezes well, which will allow you to have a stash ready for unexpected company.

1. In the bowl of a stand mixer fitted with the dough hook, mix together the sour cream, butter, sugar and salt.

2. Add yeast, water and eggs to the bowl; mix for 1 minute then add the flour and mix for 5 minutes until the dough is soft and sticky.

3. Cover and refrigerate overnight.

4. Place the dough on a lightly floured surface and cut it into thirds.

5. Divide each third into 8 pieces and roll each piece into a ball.

6. Place balls seam-side down on a greased cookie sheet.

7. Brush tops with additional melted butter.

8. Let rise for 45 minutes.

9. Preheat oven to 375 degrees.

10. Bake rolls for 15-20 minutes or until golden brown.

11. Serve warm.

Povitica

Makes 1 loaf

Ingredients

2¾ cups unbleached all purpose flour
¼ teaspoon kosher salt
1 cup water
1 tablespoon granulated sugar
¼ cup vegetable oil

1 teaspoon apple cider vinegar
2 teaspoons active dry yeast
Povitica Filling (see page 138)
Softened butter
Granulated sugar

1. In the bowl of a stand mixer fitted with the dough hook, combine flour, salt, water, sugar, oil, vinegar and yeast; mix on low for 7 minutes.

2. Apply non-stick spray to a large piece of plastic wrap and pour dough onto the wrap.

3. Spray hands with non-stick spray and pull the edges of the dough towards the center to make a tidy rectangle.

4. Fold plastic wrap over the dough and let rest for 30 minutes.

5. Apply non-stick spray to the counter and carefully invert dough onto the counter.

6. Spray hands again; pull and pat dough into a large and very thin rectangle.

7. Spread Povitica filling over the dough then roll the long top edge down to the center and roll the bottom long edge up to the center until both meet in the middle.

8. Roll the left edge to the center and the right edge to the center until they meet in the middle.

9. Invert into a greased 10-inch round cake pan; let rise for 1 hour.

10. Brush the top with butter and sprinkle with sugar; place it into the cold oven.

11. Turn oven to 350 degrees and bake for 90 minutes or until deep brown and serve.

Blackberry Croissant Bread Pudding

Makes 9 squares

Ingredients

6 croissants, day-old, split in half
1½ cups heavy cream
4 large eggs
½ cup granulated sugar
Pinch of kosher salt
1 teaspoon fresh lemon juice
1 teaspoon vanilla extract
1 cup fresh or frozen blackberries
Whipped cream

From grade 5 through grade 12, I lived in a boarding school in Kinshasa, Congo so that I could go to a school where English was both spoken and taught. Overall, it was a necessary and good experience. Some foods were good, but others, like their version of bread pudding, I simply loathed. I learned much later that the reason most people dislike bread pudding is that many people use it as an excuse to hide old, leftover or cheap ingredients. In fact, leftover or dry bread is desirable because it soaks up more of the custard which carries the flavor. So the custard part must be delicious or the whole dessert suffers. This recipe is rich and scrumptious.

1. Preheat oven to 375 degrees.

2. Place the croissants into a greased 8x8-inch pan.

3. In a bowl, combine remaining ingredients, except whipped cream; mix well.

4. Pour mixture over the croissants.

5. Let rest for 10 minutes.

6. Bake for 30-40 minutes or until custard is set.

7. Serve warm with whipped cream.

Pizza Dough

Makes two 10-inch pizzas

Ingredients

3 cups all purpose flour
1 teaspoon kosher salt
1 envelope active dry yeast
1 cup water, room temperature
1 teaspoon honey
1 tablespoon olive oil

As a chef, Wolf is probably best known for his designer pizzas. This dough recipe is the foundation for all of them. Six simple ingredients and yet it is the best crust I've ever tasted. It behaves nicely and is a joy to work with. Now that you have the dough recipe, have fun with the toppings. The sky is the limit!

Marian's Tip:
If you'd like to make your own pizza, top crust as desired then bake at 400 degrees for 12-15 minutes or until brown.

1. Fit the food processor with the metal S blade.

2. Add flour and salt into the food processor; secure lid.

3. Place remaining ingredients into a measuring cup; stir.

4. With the food processor running, pour the measuring cup contents through the feed tube and process for 30 seconds.

5. Divide the dough into 2 even balls, reserving 1 dough ball for future use.

6. Place the dough ball on a lightly floured surface and cover it with a towel; let rest for 20 minutes.

7. Stretch the dough into a 10-inch circle using floured hands.

8. Follow baking instructions for the dessert pizza (page 102).

Gluten-Free Pizza Dough

Makes two 10-inch pizzas

Ingredients

2 tablespoons olive oil
1 cup + 2 tablespoons water
⅓ cup dry potato flakes
1 cup white rice flour
½ cup tapioca flour
3 tablespoons powdered milk
1 teaspoon onion powder

1 teaspoon kosher salt
2 teaspoons xanthan gum
2 teaspoons unflavored gelatin
1 envelope dry active yeast
3 tablespoons dried egg whites
1 tablespoon granulated sugar

1. In the bowl of a stand mixer fitted with the beaters, add all ingredients in the order listed above.

2. Mix dough on medium speed for 5 minutes; stop to scrape the bowl after 2 minutes.

3. Remove the dough and let it rest for 15 minutes.

4. Shape the dough into 2 balls, reserving 1 dough ball for later use.

5. To make a pizza, pat out the dough on a oiled baking sheet using your oiled hands; let rest for 20 minutes.

6. Preheat oven to 425 degrees.

7. Bake for 15-18 minutes or until golden brown.

8. Remove and add your favorite pizza toppings.

9. Bake for an additional 12-15 minutes or until toppings are done.

Marian's Tip:
To freeze the dough, spray the inside of a quart size bag with non-stick spray then add the dough. Keep frozen for up to 3 months and thaw before using.

Dessert Pizza

Makes 1 pizza

Ingredients

Pizza dough (see page 100)
2 teaspoons unsalted butter, softened
¼ teaspoon ground cinnamon
1 tablespoon granulated sugar
½ cup cream cheese, softened
⅓ cup strawberry jam

2 kiwi fruit, peeled and sliced
1 banana, sliced
1 cup fresh strawberries, sliced
1 cup fresh blueberries
Powdered sugar

If you are having a pizza party, making this dessert pizza will put your party over the top. It is easy to make because it uses the same dough as the other pizzas. The topping tastes just like strawberry cheesecake. The fruits should be whatever varieties look best at your market that day. You don't have to be too fussy arranging the fruit. It will be beautiful and delicious.

1. Preheat oven to 400 degrees.

2. Stretch out the pizza dough.

3. Top the crust with butter, cinnamon and sugar.

4. Bake for 10-12 minutes or until golden brown.

5. While baking, combine cream cheese and jam in a bowl; mix well.

6. Spread the jam mixture over the slightly cooled crust.

7. Top pizza with kiwi, banana, strawberries and blueberries.

8. Dust with powdered sugar and serve.

Marian's Tip:
Chocolate lovers can pour 1 cup of chocolate chips over the crust when it comes out of the oven instead of using the cream cheese and jam topping. Let the chocolate stand for 2 minutes then spread it evenly with the back of a teaspoon. The heat from the crust will melt the chocolate for you.

More

Drop Donuts

Ingredients

½ cup granulated sugar
½ teaspoon kosher salt
A few gratings of fresh nutmeg
2¼ teaspoons baking powder
2 cups all purpose flour, sifted
⅓ cup whole milk

¼ cup heavy whipping cream
2 large eggs
1 teaspoon vanilla extract
1 teaspoon apple cider vinegar
6 cups vegetable oil
Powdered sugar or cinnamon sugar

Of all the homemade donut recipes, drop donuts are the easiest to make. This is because the dough is left more like a batter and is dropped into the oil by the spoonful as opposed to rolling out the dough then cutting out the circles and holes. This makes the whole process so much faster. When I get a sneaky craving for homemade donuts, this is the recipe I reach for. I am also married to a man who loves homemade donuts, so if there is ever a new cookbook or kitchen gadget that I am dying to buy, one batch of these donuts and Greg will say "yes".

1. In a large bowl, combine sugar, salt, nutmeg, baking powder and flour; whisk well.

2. Add the milk, cream, eggs, vanilla and vinegar to the bowl; stir.

3. On a stove top over medium-high heat, preheat the oil in a dutch oven until it reaches 350 degrees on a thermometer (adjust the heat to maintain this temperature).

4. Carefully drop the dough by the tablespoon into the oil.

5. Fry for 2 minutes on each side or until both sides are golden brown.

6. Drain donuts on paper towels.

7. Roll donuts in sugar and serve warm.

Marian's Tip:
Fill the donuts with the pastry cream on page 125. Use a squeeze bottle to poke a hole in the side of the donuts then squeeze in the cream.

Chocolate Cupcakes

Makes 18 cupcakes

Ingredients

1 cup unsalted butter, softened
3 cups light brown sugar, packed
4 large eggs
1 tablespoon vanilla extract
⅔ cup high quality cocoa powder
2 teaspoons baking soda
½ teaspoon kosher salt
2 cups cake flour
1½ cups sour cream
1⅓ cups water

When my boys were little and it was my turn to provide something for school class parties, this is the recipe that Jordan and Ben would beg me to make. It became quite a party in the kitchen when we were icing and using sprinkles to decorate the cupcakes, counters, cabinets and our faces. Eventually, I figured that if we were going to be having that much afternoon fun in the kitchen, there was no point in trying to make supper too. No one was ever hungry because we were always full of chocolate and sprinkles. Memories like that are priceless.

1. Prepare a cupcake pan with papers and set aside.

2. In a bowl, combine butter and sugar; cream using a hand mixer until fluffy.

3. While mixing, add the eggs (one at a time) then add the vanilla and beat until smooth.

4. Sift the cocoa powder, baking soda, salt and flour. Slowly add them to the bowl, alternating with the sour cream and water until all ingredients have been added. Mix until smooth.

5. Using an ice cream scoop, place batter into the cupcake papers until 3/4 full.

6. Preheat oven to 350 degrees.

7. Bake for 20 minutes or until puffed and set.

8. Let cool completely.

9. Fill and frost as desired before serving.

Vanilla Cupcakes

Makes 24 cupcakes

Ingredients

3 cups cake flour
1½ cups all purpose flour
¾ teaspoon baking soda
2¼ teaspoons baking powder
2 teaspoons kosher salt
1 cup + 2 tablespoons unsalted butter

2⅓ cups granulated sugar
5 large eggs
3 large egg yolks
2 cups buttermilk
1 tablespoon vanilla extract
½ teaspoon butter-vanilla extract

When Wolf decided that he wanted to sell a cupcake mix on HSN, he asked me to come up with recipes for him to test. To get an idea of what he expected, he mailed me a box of his favorite cupcakes from an upscale bakery in Beverly Hills. When the box arrived, I just smiled. Only Wolf would mail a box like this. Instead of using packing peanuts, he cushioned the box with 3 fine linen table cloths and 10 napkins from Spago. He used "homemade" ice packs of zipper top bags that now just contained water leaking all over the box. When I unwrapped each of the 12 varieties of cupcakes, I started laughing. Wolf had taken a bite out of each one! This recipe is similar to the vanilla cupcake he mailed to me which is his favorite.

1. Preheat oven to 350 degrees.

2. Prepare a cupcake pan with papers and set aside.

3. In a bowl, sift together the flours, baking soda, baking powder and salt.

4. In a separate bowl, combine butter and sugar; cream using a hand mixer until fluffy.

5. While mixing on medium speed, add the eggs (one at a time) then add the egg yolks.

6. While mixing, add the flour mixture and buttermilk in batches, alternating between the two until incorporated.

7. Add the extracts and mix to incorporate.

8. Using an ice cream scoop, place batter into the cupcake papers until 3/4 full.

9. Bake for 20 minutes or until golden brown.

10. Let cool then fill and frost as desired before serving.

Vanilla Panna Cotta

Makes 4 servings

Ingredients

½ vanilla bean, preferably Tahitian, split in half lengthwise (see source page 141)

1½ cups heavy cream

½ cup whole milk

1½ teaspoons powdered, unflavored gelatin (exact measure necessary)

2 tablespoons water

⅓ cup sugar

A few grains of kosher salt

Italian for cooked cream, Panna Cotta is like the best Crème Brûlée but without the eggy taste as it doesn't contain eggs. Even though I consider eggs to be the most wondrous of all the ingredients in the world of baking, I do not eat them by themselves. Whether you like eggs or not, this silky custard is sublime all by itself, with the sweet cream flavor and lovely undertones from the vanilla bean. This is a recipe where you really need to use vanilla beans. Vanilla extract just can't provide the correct vanilla flavor.

1. In a microwave-safe bowl, combine the vanilla bean, heavy cream and milk.

2. Microwave for 2 minutes or until very hot.

3. Let rest for 10 minutes, stirring occasionally.

4. Pour the cream mixture through a strainer and remove the vanilla bean; set aside.

5. In a small cup, combine gelatin and water; stir and let rest for 5 minutes then microwave until hot.

6. Add the gelatin mixture to the cream mixture then add the sugar and salt; stir.

7. Divide between four dessert glasses.

8. Chill for 3 hours or until set before serving.

Marian's Tip:
For red and white Panna Cotta, divide the cream mixture created in step 6. Stir 1/4 cup strawberry purée into half of the mixture. Layer into the dessert glasses by alternating the white and red mixture, chilling between adding another layer.

Silky Vanilla Crème Caramel

Makes 6 servings

Caramel Ingredients

½ cup granulated sugar
¼ cup light corn syrup
1 drop fresh lemon juice

Vanilla Custard

1 cup whole milk
1 cup heavy cream
⅔ cup granulated sugar
Pinch of kosher salt
1 teaspoon excellent quality pure vanilla extract
2 large eggs
3 large egg yolks

1. Combine all caramel ingredients in a 4-cup microwave-safe glass measuring cup; stir until the sugar is moistened.

2. Microwave on high for 3 minutes or until bubbles form and the color changes to a light amber.

3. Remove and swirl until color changes to a medium amber then quickly divide the mixture between six ungreased 4-ounce ramekins; tilt and swirl each ramekin to distribute the caramel across the bottom and halfway up the sides of each ramekin then set aside.

4. To make the custard, preheat oven to 275 degrees.

5. Place a folded kitchen towel inside a baking pan with sides.

6. Add 1½ cups of water to the pan and place it inside the oven.

7. In a bowl, combine all custard ingredients; whisk until smooth.

8. Divide mixture between the caramel-lined ramekins.

9. Carefully place the ramekins on the towel-lined pan in the oven.

10. Bake for 40 minutes or until the custard jiggles like gelatin and a knife inserted off center comes out clean.

11. Remove and chill for at least 2 hours.

12. To serve, run a thin knife around the edge of each ramekin and invert onto plates with rims; when lifting off the ramekins, let the caramel drip over the custard.

Crème Brûlée

Makes 6 servings

Ingredients

2 cups heavy cream
1 vanilla bean, split
½ cup granulated sugar

7 large egg yolks
Additional sugar for burning the tops

1. Preheat oven to 275 degrees.

2. In a saucepan over medium heat, combine cream and vanilla bean; bring to a simmer (bubbles will form around the edges of the pan) then remove from heat and let rest for 10 minutes.

3. In a bowl, combine the sugar and egg yolks; mix until smooth.

4. Pour the cream mixture through a strainer into the sugar mixture; whisk well.

5. Place 6 ramekins inside a baking pan with sides.

6. Divide mixture between the ramekins and fill almost to the top of each ramekin.

7. Carefully pour 1 inch of hot water into the baking pan around the ramekins.

8. Place pan in the oven and bake for 30 minutes or until set but still pale in color.

9. Remove from the oven and refrigerate for at least 1 hour.

10. Place each crème brûlée on a cookie sheet.

11. Sprinkle each crème brûlée top with an even layer of sugar.

12. Using a blow torch (see tools on page 9), burn the tops to caramelize the sugar.

13. Sprinkle a second layer of sugar and burn to caramelize again.

14. Allow to stand for 5 minutes before serving.

Dark Chocolate Crème Brûlée

Makes 4 servings

Ingredients

1½ cups heavy whipping cream
⅓ cup semi-sweet chocolate chips
½ teaspoon pure vanilla extract
2 tablespoons granulated sugar
5 large egg yolks
Microwave Caramel (see page 126)

1. Heat the cream in a microwave-safe bowl for 1-2 minutes or until hot.

2. Add the chocolate chips to the cream; whisk until the chocolate is melted.

3. Whisk in remaining ingredients, except microwave caramel, until completely combined.

4. Preheat oven to 300 degrees.

5. Pour 1 inch of hot water into a large pan with 2-inch sides.

6. Place four 6-ounce ramekins in the pan holding the water.

7. Divide the mixture between the ramekins and bake for 30 minutes.

8. To test for doneness, insert the tip of a small knife slightly off the center of the ramekin. If the knife comes out clean, it's done. If it is not clean, cook for an additional 5 minutes.

9. Cover and chill for a minimum of 1 hour.

10. Just before serving, pour a thin layer of microwave caramel over the top.

Marian's Tip:
You can also brown the tops by sprinkling granulated sugar and using a blow torch (see the bottom of page 112).

Simple Chocolate Soufflés

Makes 4 servings

Ingredients

½ cup excellent quality semi-sweet chocolate chips
½ cup heavy whipping cream
4 large egg whites
2 tablespoons granulated sugar

Four ingredients is all you need to make this recipe. Soufflés get way more than their share of "oohs and ahhs" in the restaurant. They do take some last-minute mixing and baking but they certainly are not difficult to make. This one is chocolaty, tender, fluffy and decadent. The sauce poured over them provides an unbelievable contrast to the crispy exterior. Make sure your guests are ready to eat these the moment they come out of the oven so they can appreciate these puffed up soufflés before they deflate.

1. Butter and sugar the inside of four 6-ounce ramekins.

2. Place the ramekins on a baking sheet.

3. Place the chocolate and cream into a microwave-safe bowl.

4. Microwave for 2 minutes or until mixture is hot and chocolate is melted; stir until smooth.

5. Divide mixture into 2 separate bowls, cover and cool.

6. In the bowl of a stand mixer fitted with the whip attachment, beat egg whites on medium until foamy.

7. While mixing, gradually add the sugar until soft peaks form (the peaks should curl over).

8. Gently fold one bowl of the chocolate mixture into the egg whites until combined.

9. Spoon into prepared ramekins.

10. Preheat oven to 400 degrees.

11. Bake for 15-18 minutes or until soufflés have risen above the rim of the ramekins.

12. Top with remaining chocolate mixture and serve.

Raspberry Soufflés

Makes 6 servings

Ingredients

2 tablespoons unsalted butter
2 tablespoons granulated sugar for sprinkling
5 large egg whites
¼ teaspoon cream of tartar
⅔ cup granulated sugar
1 tablespoon cornstarch
½ cup raspberries, puréed
Powdered sugar
1 cup Raspberry Coulis (see page 137)

These are the exact raspberry soufflés we bake in all of the convection airings on HSN. Simple ingredients and the magic of egg whites is really all there is to a soufflé.

1. Preheat oven to 400 degrees.

2. Butter and sprinkle sugar on 6 straight-sided ramekins; place them on a baking sheet.

3. In a bowl, whisk egg whites on medium speed using a hand mixer fitted with the whisk attachment.

4. When egg whites become foamy, add the cream of tartar then slowly add the sugar; beat until soft peaks form and the tips curl over.

5. Gently fold in the cornstarch and raspberries.

6. Divide the mixture between the ramekins and fill to mound slightly; clean rims using your finger.

7. Bake for 7-10 minutes or until well risen and brown on top.

8. Dust with powdered sugar and serve immediately topped with Raspberry Coulis.

Popovers

Makes 6 servings

Ingredients

¾ cup whole milk
3 large eggs
2 teaspoons powdered sugar
½ teaspoon kosher salt
¾ cup all purpose flour

When you make these popovers, pull up a chair and watch them rise through the oven window. It is quite a sight. Because the batter has so much liquid and eggs in it, the steam that is created in the hot oven causes them to swell dramatically. When they are finished baking, you will have a lovely puffed top that is brown and crispy. This will give way to a moist, creamy and eggy interior. My family likes these best served with roast beef and gravy.

1. Move the oven rack to the lower part of the oven.

2. Preheat oven to 400 degrees.

3. In a pitcher, combine all ingredients; mix well using an immersion blender (batter will be very thin).

4. Coat a 6-cup popover pan with vegetable oil and place it in the oven to preheat.

5. Open the oven door and carefully pour the batter into each well until each is 2/3 filled.

6. Bake for 30 minutes or until the popovers are deep brown and a few inches taller than the pan.

7. Serve immediately as they will deflate quickly.

Marian's Tip:
I often add chives to the batter before baking.

Zesty Lime Gelato

Ingredients
Zest from 3 limes
4 tablespoons fresh lime juice
⅔ cup granulated sugar
1 cup heavy whipping cream
1 cup plain whole milk yogurt
1 teaspoon pure vanilla extract
Pinch of kosher salt

1. In a bowl, combine all ingredients; whisk until smooth.

2. Chill for 4 hours or until very cold.

3. Spin in an ice cream machine according to the manufacturer's instructions. If you do not have an ice cream machine, freeze solid in a covered container then chop and pulse in a food processor until just smooth.

4. Remove and transfer to an airtight container and freeze for 2 hours before serving.

5. Gelato will keep for up to 3 days.

Marian's Tip:
Serve this gelato with the Honey Tuile Cookies on page 48.

Kiwi Sorbet

Makes about 1 quart

Ingredients

10 large kiwi fruit, peeled and puréed
½ cup granulated sugar

It's hard to believe that 2 ingredients can make a sorbet but it is true. The secret lies in the fruit. If the fruit is ripe and very fragrant, it will most certainly make excellent sorbet. Even fruits that I normally don't like to eat, such as cantaloupe, taste delicious when made into a sorbet. You can use this same recipe to make sorbet from the fruit you like best. I prefer sorbet over ice cream and love making this treat any day of the week. A Farmer's Market is a wonderful place to find good, ripe fruit.

1. In a bowl, combine all ingredients; mix well.

2. Taste and add sugar if necessary until the mixture tastes just slightly too sweet.

3. Pour mixture into a shallow container.

4. Cover and freeze.

5. Once frozen, remove and break it up into small chunks using a fork.

6. Add the chunks to a food processor fitted with the metal S blade.

7. Secure lid and pulse until smooth and creamy.

8. Quickly remove and freeze again until ready to eat.

9. This sorbet can be frozen for up to 5 days.

Grapefruit Sorbet

Makes 4 cups

Ingredients

10 Ruby Red grapefruits
⅔ cup granulated sugar
A few drops of red food coloring (optional)

Of all the ice creams and sorbets I have ever made for Wolf, this one is by far his absolute favorite. Even people who really aren't crazy about grapefruit love it. It's refreshing in taste and has a HUGE flavor. When we sold an electric ice cream machine on HSN, Wolf would look for this sorbet and just eat it by the spoonful right out of the bucket. I don't think he ever really tasted the other 10 flavors I had out there. When the segment was over, he would take the little pail out of the machine and carry it with him to the next item we were selling. Now you can make it yourself and see just how incredibly simple it is to make. I add a drop of red food coloring to mine because the color makes me happy.

1. Zest 5 of the grapefruits.

2. Juice all of the grapefruits.

3. Strain the juice to remove any seeds.

4. In a bowl, combine zest, juice and sugar.

5. Add additional sugar to adjust the sweetness as desired.

6. Add food coloring if desired.

7. Refrigerate until very cold.

8. Spin in your ice cream maker according to the manufacturer's instructions (if you don't have an ice cream maker, just cover and freeze).

9. Once frozen, chop it into chunks and pulse it in the food processor until solid.

10. Serve immediately.

Fillings & Toppings

Pastry Cream

Makes 2 - 3 cups

Ingredients

½ cup sugar
¼ cup cornstarch
Pinch of kosher salt
4 large egg yolks
2 cups half & half
1 vanilla bean

Pastry cream is like really good vanilla pudding. It is easy to make and very versatile. Use it to fill any of the cakes you choose to make. It can also be used as the base for any cream pie, a filling for donuts, cream puffs or éclairs. Because it is delicately flavored, this is a good time to use real vanilla beans or pure vanilla extract.

Marian's Tip:
If you don't have a vanilla bean handy, just use a teaspoon of pure vanilla extract.

1. In a medium saucepan, combine sugar, cornstarch, salt and egg yolks; whisk well.

2. Do not turn on the stove yet.

3. In a microwave-safe bowl, microwave the half & half and vanilla bean until very hot.

4. While whisking the sugar mixture in the saucepan very fast, slowly pour in the half & half mixture.

5. Turn on the stove to medium heat.

6. Whisk steadily, scraping all over until the mixture comes to a full boil.

7. Remove from heat then discard the vanilla bean.

8. Transfer the cream to a container and press a piece of plastic wrap directly onto the cream's surface to prevent a skin from forming.

9. Chill before using it to fill cakes or as desired.

Microwave Caramel

Ingredients

½ cup granulated sugar
2 tablespoons water
¼ cup light corn syrup
1 drop fresh lemon juice or vinegar

Making caramel in the microwave is so much easier than on the stove top. This is the easiest way I know of to top crème brûlée, unless of course you own a blow torch.

1. In a 4-cup glass measuring cup, combine all ingredients.

2. Stir until the sugar is moistened.

3. Microwave on high for 3 minutes.

4. Watch for the bubbles to start piling up in the cup.

5. When the color changes to a light amber, carefully remove the cup from the microwave.

6. Swirl the cup until the color turns to a medium amber.

7. Use quickly before caramel hardens.

Marian's Tip:
To remove any hardened caramel from the measuring cup, pour 1 inch of water into the cup. Microwave it for a minute then carefully lift out the melted caramel with a fork and discard it.

Real Toasted Coconut

Makes 4 cups

Ingredients

1 fresh coconut, heavy for its size and full of liquid
¼ cup granulated sugar
⅛ teaspoon pure coconut extract

When I was little, I could scamper up a coconut palm and twist off the big nuts like it was nothing. I bet if I were to try that today, I could not climb 3 feet off the ground. Back then, my favorite thing to make with coconut was coconut cream pie because my dad liked it best. When I came to America and first tasted the coconuts available at the grocery store, I was shocked and disappointed. Store bought coconut sold in bags in the baking aisle tastes nothing like it should. My advice is to just make it yourself. It's so easy. When buying coconuts, make sure they are full of liquid, feel heavy for their size and that the 3 "eyes" located on one of the ends are not moldy or wet.

1. Using an ice pick or nail, pierce one of the soft "eyes" of the coconut.

2. Shake out the coconut water into a bowl or discard it.

3. Using a hammer, pound the coconut shell around the center until it cracks into 3 or 4 pieces.

4. Using a butter knife, pry the coconut flesh out of the hard shell and discard the shell.

5. Rinse off the coconut meat but do not peel off the brown exterior.

6. Using a vegetable peeler, peel coconut into strips.

7. Preheat oven to 300 degrees.

8. In a bowl, combine coconut strips, sugar and extract; toss until coated.

9. Spread out the coconut strips onto aluminum foil lined cookie sheets.

10. Bake for 20 minutes then stir the coconut.

11. Rotate the cookie sheets and continue baking for 10-20 minutes or until golden brown and crispy.

Spun Sugar

Makes several dozen

Ingredients

Microwave Caramel (see page 126)

Of all the garnishes I have used at the restaurant, none have gotten as much attention as spun sugar. It is as fun to make as it is beautiful to look at. Play around with it until you make just the garnish you like. If you live in a humid area like I do, make little packets of silica gel out of a paper towel and a rubber band and store your creations in a well sealed container with the silica gel. You can find silica gel in the fresh flower preserving section of the craft store. I learned to make this beautiful garnish from Sherry Yard, Wolf's pastry chef at Spago.

1. Fill a large bowl with ice water.

2. Cover a 3 foot area of the countertop and floor with a tablecloth.

3. Place the handle of a pan so that it protrudes past the countertop to catch the sugar.

4. Prepare the Microwave Caramel.

5. Dip a fork into the caramel and stir gently.

6. When the mixture starts to be thick like honey, pick up a fork full and let some of it fall back into the cup. If it falls in long threads, it is ready to use. If it drips, it is still too hot.

7. Dip the fork into the caramel, pull it up and with a sharp wrist action, shake the fork back and forth (away from your body) over the protruding pan handle to produce long, golden threads.

8. Gather up all the threads and shape them into a loose ball; immediately place the ball into a dry, airtight container.

9. Repeat until you have your desired amount.

10. Use the spun sugar within an hour.

Seven Minute Frosting

Makes 5 cups

Ingredients

2 large egg whites
2 tablespoons light corn syrup
1½ cups granulated sugar
5 tablespoons water
¼ teaspoon cream of tartar
⅛ teaspoon kosher salt
1 teaspoon pure vanilla extract
⅛ teaspoon butter-vanilla extract

1. Fashion a double boiler out of a pot containing 2 inches of water and a metal or glass mixing bowl; nest the bowl comfortably in the pot without having the bottom of the bowl touch the water.

2. Bring the water in the double boiler to a simmer over medium heat.

3. In the double boiler, combine all ingredients, except the vanilla and butter-vanilla extracts.

4. Using a hand mixer, mix on medium speed for a few seconds until moistened.

5. Increase speed to high and whip for 7 minutes or until very billowy and peaks form.

6. Add the extracts and mix just to incorporate.

7. Use the frosting immediately as it will form a crust after about 15 minutes.

8. This icing is typically piled on cakes quite thickly then swirled into waves and peaks using the back of a spoon.

Marian's Tip:
Try this frosting on the vanilla cupcakes on page 107.

Royal Icing Glaze

Makes 2 cups

Ingredients

3½ cups powdered sugar, sifted
2 large egg whites

1 teaspoon fresh lemon juice
Water to thin the glaze

This is the magic glaze for decorating cookies. Once dry, you can stack the cookies as the glaze will remain perfectly flat. You can also color the glaze any way you want using food coloring. The secret to the glaze is to have all the colors come from the same batch so they are the same thickness. Also, try to have the same number of food coloring drops in each color. If the glazes all have the same viscosity, they stay put on the cookie until you move them to create beautiful designs. See some examples on page 43. This is also the same glaze I use on Napoleons or to glaze pound cakes. It is also the perfect "glue" for building gingerbread houses. It can be kept, tightly covered at room temperature for up to 1 week.

1. In a bowl, combine the sugar, egg whites and lemon juice; stir using a teaspoon.

2. Add enough water to make a pourable glaze (about 1 teaspoon).

3. To test, pour a teaspoon of glaze into a saucer. It should be moveable but stand in a tall puddle with a very defined border.

4. If it is too thick, add some additional lemon juice, if it is too thin, add some additional powdered sugar.

5. To use the icing, fill a parchment cone with icing and use as desired.

6. Keep the icing covered at all times when it is not being used.

Marian's Tip:
For a different color icing, just add some food coloring.

Swiss Meringue

Makes about 6 cups

Ingredients

4 large egg whites
1 cup granulated sugar
½ teaspoon vanilla extract

1. Wash hands, bowl, mixer whisks, anything that will come in contact with the egg whites as any form of grease, even a bit of egg yolk will prevent the mixture from getting fluffy and stiff.

2. In a double boiler or a metal bowl nested in a saucepot containing 1 inch of simmering water, combine egg whites and sugar; whisk gently until all sugar grains have dissolved and mixture is warm but not hot.

3. Pour the mixture into a bowl.

4. Using a hand mixer, beat the mixture on high speed for several minutes until stiff peaks form.

5. Add the vanilla extract and beat briefly to incorporate.

6. Swiss Meringue is only workable for about 8 minutes before it sets and looks curdled.

Lemon Curd

Makes about 3 cups

Ingredients

¾ cup granulated sugar

2 tablespoons lemon zest

¾ cup fresh lemon juice

6 large egg yolks

¾ cup unsalted butter, cubed

2 teaspoons additional lemon zest

Lemon curd is one of the best fillings I know of. It's silky, seductive and easy to make. Adding a portion of the lemon zest at the end when the mixture has cooled is well worth the effort. This last bit of zest is not cooked so it retains a brighter, cleaner taste.

1. Fashion a double boiler out of a pot containing 2 inches of water and a metal or glass mixing bowl; nest the bowl comfortably in the pot without having the bottom of the bowl touch the water.

2. In the bowl, combine sugar, 2 tablespoons of lemon zest, lemon juice and egg yolks; whisk slowly.

3. Over medium-high heat, stir gently for 5-8 minutes or until mixture is too hot to touch and has thickened significantly.

4. Pour mixture through a fine strainer.

5. Cool for 5 minutes then whisk in the butter until melted and smooth.

6. Whisk in the remaining lemon zest.

7. Store in an airtight container for up to 2 weeks or freeze for up to 2 months.

Marian's Tip:
To turn this recipe into Passion Fruit Curd called for in the Pavlova recipe on page 74, omit the lemon juice and zest. Simply substitute 3/4 cup of unsweetened passion fruit juice.

Homemade Marshmallows

Makes 60 marshmallows

Ingredients

2 cups cornstarch, divided

2 tablespoons unflavored gelatin

3 tablespoons water

1⅔ cups granulated sugar

1½ cups light corn syrup

⅔ cup water

3 large egg whites

2 teaspoons vanilla extract

1 teaspoon butter vanilla extract

A few drops of food coloring (optional)

1. Sift an even layer of cornstarch over a 1/2 sheet pan; set aside.

2. In the bowl of a stand mixer, combine gelatin and 3 tablespoons of water.

3. Whisk fast to moisten the gelatin before it thickens; let stand for 5 minutes.

4. In a 4-quart saucepan over medium-high heat, combine sugar, corn syrup and remaining water; heat for 8 minutes or until 242 degrees on a thermometer.

5. Immediately pour the hot syrup over the gelatin in the stand mixer bowl.

6. Turn the mixer on low speed then on high speed and mix for 5 minutes.

7. Add remaining ingredients, except remaining cornstarch, and mix until the mixture quadruples in volume (add food coloring if desired).

8. Scrape the marshmallow mixture onto the prepared 1/2 sheet pan.

9. Sift a layer of cornstarch over the top and let cool for 2 hours.

10. Sift a thin layer of cornstarch over a large cutting board.

11. Using your fingers, pry the sheet of marshmallow from the pan and place it on the cutting board.

12. Using a knife, trim the edges and cut it into even squares.

13. Roll marshmallows in cornstarch, shake off the excess and serve.

Chocolate Glaze

Ingredients

4 ounces semi-sweet chocolate chips
3 tablespoons unsalted butter
3 tablespoons whole milk
1½ cups powdered sugar

1. In a microwave-safe bowl, combine chocolate chips and butter.

2. Microwave until melted.

3. Stir until smooth then stir in remaining ingredients.

Vanilla Glaze

Ingredients

1¼ cups powdered sugar
2 tablespoons water
¼ teaspoon pure vanilla extract

1. In a bowl, combine all ingredients; stir until smooth.

2. Keep covered until ready to use.

Quick Strawberry Mousse Filling

Ingredients

½ cup fresh strawberries
½ cup powdered sugar
1½ cups heavy cream, cold

1. In a narrow mixing bowl, combine all ingredients.

2. Using an immersion blender, whip until the mousse is thick and fluffy.

3. Don't overmix or the cream will curdle.

Raspberry Coulis

Ingredients

1 bag (12 ounces) frozen raspberries, thawed
⅔ cup granulated sugar

1. Using a blender or food processor, purée ingredients until very smooth.

2. Strain through a fine strainer to remove seeds if desired.

Apple Strudel Filling

Ingredients

4 Granny Smith apples, peeled, halved and very thinly sliced
4 Pink Lady apples, peeled, halved and very thinly sliced
1 cup granulated sugar
2 tablespoons fresh lemon juice
2 teaspoons ground cinnamon
2 tablespoons tapioca flour
Pinch of kosher salt

1. In a large bowl, combine all ingredients.

2. Let rest for 45 minutes, stirring occasionally.

3. Drain any juices and continue to follow instructions on page 78.

Povitica Filling

Ingredients

2 large eggs, beaten
3 cups toasted walnuts or pecans
1 cup poppy seeds
1 cup granulated sugar

3 tablespoons all purpose flour
1 tablespoon ground cinnamon
½ teaspoon ground cardamom

1. Brush eggs evenly over the rolled out Povitica dough (see page 96).

2. In a bowl, combine remaining ingredients and sprinkle over the dough.

3. Spread filling and pat to help it adhere to the dough.

Blue Cheese & Grape Topping

Ingredients

2 tablespoons fresh rosemary leaves
⅓ cup blue cheese, crumbled
1 cup red seedless grapes
2 tablespoons honey

1. Prepare the dough for the Basic Focaccia bread (see page 92).

2. Before baking the dough, top it with the above ingredients.

3. Continue baking as directed in the Focaccia bread recipe.

Chocolate Ganache Icing

Ingredients

2½ cups heavy cream
2 cups semi-sweet chocolate chips
1 teaspoon vanilla extract

1. In a microwave-safe bowl, heat the cream until bubbles form around the edges.

2. Add chocolate and vanilla to the hot cream; let rest for 1 minute.

3. Whisk until smooth and all the chocolate has melted.

4. Let rest for 1 hour or until thick before spreading it on a cake.

Banana Jam

Ingredients

4 overripe bananas, mashed
1 cup granulated sugar
2 teaspoons fresh lemon juice

1. In a saucepan over medium heat, combine all ingredients.

2. Bring to a boil, stirring occasionally; boil for 5 minutes.

3. Let cool before using.

Colored Decorator Sugar

Ingredients

1 cup granulated sugar
6 drops food coloring of your choice

1. In a plastic zipper bag, combine all ingredients; close the bag.

2. Shake vigorously until sugar is uniformly colored.

3. If darker color spots remain, press the bag between your fingers to incorporate the color into the sugar then shake again.

4. Decorate cookies as desired.

Source Page

Chocosphere
P.O. Box 2237, Tualatin, OR 97062
(877) 992-4626
www.chocosphere.com

excellent quality cocoa (Callebaut), chocolates, jimmies and sprinkles

The Bakers Catalogue at King Arthur Flour
135 Route 5 South, Norwich, VT 05055
(800) 827-6836
www.kingarthurflour.com

flours, pure fruit oils, citric acid, baker's ammonia, blow torches, kitchen tools, baking pans

Penzeys Spices
12001 W. Capitol Drive, Wauwatosa, WI 53222
(800) 741-7787
www.penzeys.com

spices, extracts, seasonings & more

Gluten Free Mall
4927 Sonoma Hwy, Ste C1, Santa Rosa, CA 65409
(866) 575-3720
www.glutenfreemall.com

all ingredients needed for gluten-free baking

D&G Occansions
625 Herndon Ave, Orlando, FL 32803
(407) 894-4458
www.dandgoccasions.com

butter-vanilla extract by Magic Line, citric acid, pure fruit oils, candy making and baking supplies

Nui Enterprises
501 Chapala St, Suite A, Santa Barbara, CA 93101
(805) 965-5153
www.vanillafromtahiti.com

pure vanilla extracts and high quality vanilla beans

Whole Foods
550 Bowie St., Austin, TX 78703
(512) 499-4455
www.wholefoodsmarket.com

grains, citric acid, natural and organic products, xanthan gum, gluten-free baking items

Fortune Products Inc.
205 Hickory Creek Rd., Marble Falls, TX 78654
(830) 693-61111
www.accusharp.com

hand-held Accusharp knife sharpeners

Rolling Pin Kitchen Emporium
P.O. Box 21798, Long Beach, CA 90801
customerservice@rollingpin.com
www.rollingpin.com

baker's ammonia, cheesecloths, kitchen tools

Index